EPHESIANS

Pattern for Christian Living

RAY SUMMERS

BROADMAN PRESS
Nashville, Tennessee

ISBN: 0-8054-1345-6

4213-45

Dewey Decimal Classification Number: 227.5
Library of Congress Catalog Card Number: 60-5195
Printed in the United States of America

Preface

Basically there are two doctrines in the New Testament: how to be saved—that is, justification by grace through faith plus nothing; and how the saved ought to live. Comprehensively, this covers the New Testament. In a very real sense, every other doctrine is properly placed in one of these categories. As an expression of basic Christianity the epistle to the Ephesians stands near the top in any consideration of doctrine and ethics. This was true in the day when Christianity was a young and growing movement. It is equally true in the twentieth century when Christianity has come to be one of the major forces challenging the minds and the loyalties of men.

For this reason the epistle to the Ephesians has a particular relevance today. No loftier expression can be found than that which is presented in this epistle. Everywhere and in multiple ways man is seeking for "the good life." Many movements—religious, social, political—offer their way to the realization of the good life. It is at this point that Christianity steps forward to present its own challenge to the best thinking and the best living for every man. When that challenge is reduced to its basic minimum or lowest common denominator, these are the elements which remain: the way of salvation; the presentation of that way to men; the application of that way in life, whether in individual or group activity. Ephesians is the loftiest expression of this basic minimum to be found in the New Testament.

The purpose of the work before us is to present a guide to the understanding of this relevant message in both its doctrinal and ethical implications. In the New Testament there can be no division of the two—doctrine and ethics. For purposes of organization the Epistles do at times set out, first, a doctrinal section and, second, an ethical section showing how this doctrinal truth is to be applied in the lives of men.[1] This, however, is a matter of organization and presentation only. The writers of the New Testament would never have thought of putting doctrine in one pigeonhole and ethics in another, as though the two were separate matters. They are the two sides of one picture, and that is the total Christian approach to life. This study will be for the most part nontechnical in nature. The Greek text of Ephesians will be in the background of the study at every point, but there will be a determined effort to present the material in such a way that the reader who has no acquaintance with Greek will experience no handicap in understanding the interpretation. It is the hope of the author that the study will be useful not only for college and seminary students and pastors but also for the great mass of laymen who hunger for an understanding of the New Testament and seek nontechnical source material for arriving at that understanding.

In line with this purpose certain limitations must be placed upon the work. There are several areas of research

[1] For this pattern, compare Ephesians: doctrine, 1–3; application, 4–6. Romans: doctrine, 1–11; application, 12–16. Galatians: doctrine, 1–4; application, 5–6. Colossians: doctrine, 1–2; application, 3–4. 1 Peter: doctrine, 1:1 to 2:10; application, 2:11 to 5:14. Hebrews: doctrine, 1:1 to 10:18; application, 10:19 to 13:25.

related to every book in the New Testament which offer stimulating and fascinating consideration to the one who desires to explore them. Ample source material for such approach is available and will be found in the bibliography at the end of this book. The bibliography is of such nature that it will guide the individual who desires to pursue these problems of research and to come to an understanding of the views of the scholars, whether of liberal or conservative approach. One of the areas of research not included in this study is that of the authorship of the epistle to the Ephesians. The claim is made that the epistle was written by the apostle Paul. This was the traditional position through all the years when the different Christian writings were being used by the churches as the processes of canonization were being worked out. In fact, the Pauline authorship of the book was unchallenged for centuries. In the bibliography at the end of this book are many works on New Testament introduction. These include works by those who accept the Pauline authorship of the book and those who reject such authorship. The evidences leading to the conclusion of the particular author are presented. For my own part, I have studied every argument available on both sides of the controversy and, recognizing that among the scholars it is still a subject of controversy, I feel no hesitation in accepting the traditional view that the book was written by the apostle Paul.

Another area of research relates to the problem of the date of the book. This in turn is inevitably tied in with the problems of place of writing and authorship. The author presents himself in the epistle as a prisoner. In considering Paul as the author of the book, two outstanding prison experiences appear in the book of Acts. Another appears when one accepts 2 Timothy as a genuine letter from Paul. Paul was in prison when he wrote 2 Timothy, but it appears to be an imprisonment not found in his lifetime as presented in the book of Acts. In Acts we find Paul a prisoner for two years in Jerusalem and Caesarea (Acts 21:27 to 26:32) and two years in Rome (Acts 27:1 to 28:31). The pastoral epistles in the order of their writing (1 Timothy, Titus, and 2 Timothy) appear to present missionary activity of Paul after that first Roman imprisonment and ending with the second Roman imprisonment. This makes three notable prison experiences during which time the letter could have been written. Some authorities feel that the conditions behind the Ephesian letter suggest Caesarea as the more probable place of writing. If this is correct, the date of writing would be perhaps A.D. 58 or 59, depending on the chronology which one uses for the life of Paul. Most of the authorities who accept Pauline authorship, however, hold that the letter was written from the first Roman imprisonment, which would place it somewhere in the A.D. 60–62 period. A person's chronology of the life of Paul depends much on the date which he fixes for the conversion of Paul and his understanding of Paul's references to two trips to Jerusalem in Galatians 1:18 and 2:1. Again, my own study of the arguments and evidences leaves me with the impression that the most probable place of writing is Rome during Paul's first Roman imprisonment, with the period from A.D. 60 to early 62 as the date covering that imprisonment.

One of the most vexing problems for the scholars has to do with the recipients of the epistle. On the surface that might appear to be a superficial problem, since the letter itself is addressed to "the saints who are in Ephesus" (1:1). That salutation, however, does not solve the problem with the ease of similar salutations in Romans, Corinthians, Thessalonians, and Colossians. There are several problems involved in the matter of recipients. One that must head the list is the fact that in the best Greek manuscripts on Ephesians the expression "in Ephesus" is not found. It is absent from Sinaiticus, Vaticanus, the Chester Beatty Papyri, 67[2], 424[2], and 1739[2]. It is also clear that the expression was absent from Marcion's Canon, and both Tertullian and Origen indicate that it was absent from the manuscripts which they used. It is included in Alexandrinus, Bezae, and in the old Latin and Syriac versions. In the science of textual studies such evidence is regarded as conclusive that the expression was not in the earliest circulated copies of the epistle and most likely was not in the original.

This likelihood suggests the possibility that Paul wrote the epistle as a general treatise to be used as a circular letter for all the churches in Asia Minor. Wherever the letter was read, the name of the church would be inserted in the public reading: Ephesus, Colossae, Laodicea, etc. In fact, in Colossians 4:16 Paul instructed the Colossians to send their epistle (Colossians) for reading in the church at Laodicea; they in turn were to read the epistle which would come to them from Laodicea. The term used is not "to Laodicea" but "from Laodicea," leaving the impression that it was a letter which was in circulation and, having been read at Laodicea, would find Colossae as its next destination.

There are other reasons for thinking that the epistle entitled "Ephesians" may have been a circular letter. In Colossians 4:7–8 and Ephesians 6:21–22 reference is made to Tychicus as going on a general mission of instruction. Tychicus appears to have been the bearer of the specific letter to the Colossians, and he was probably the bearer of this circular letter which Paul wanted all the churches to hear. There was a particular problem in the church at Colossae which called for a particular letter. The Ephesian letter faces up to no such specific problem; rather, it is general and not local in tone, in salutation, in conclusion, as well as throughout the discussion. There is evidence, too, from Ephesians 1:15 and 3:2 that many of the readers of the epistle were not personally acquainted with Paul. This is understandable, if the letter was to be used throughout Asia Minor. It is difficult to understand if the letter was directed only to Ephesus, where Paul had spent three years in ministry.

This discussion is merely suggestive of the lengthy lines of argument and evidence to be found in sources previously cited. To me it appears that we have excellent position for understanding and appreciating the message of this epistle if we think of it in terms of a circular letter written by the apostle Paul from his imprisonment in Rome and sent for the purpose of reading in Ephesus but also in Colossae, Laodicea, and other churches of that strategic center of the Christian movement. It is Paul's finest expression of Christianity at its basic best, the way to the good life.

Contents

Introduction

In its earliest years Christianity had some introduction in Asia. It is impossible to know anything of the extent or effectiveness of this earliest introduction. Luke makes specific note of the fact that among those who heard the Christian message preached at Pentecost there were representatives from Asia (Acts 2:9). Paul introduced the gospel to some parts of the peninsula in his preaching in the territory of Cilicia as early as A.D. 40–43. A few years later, perhaps A.D. 44–48 or 49, Paul engaged in rather extensive missionary work farther west in Perga, Antioch, Iconium, Lystra, and Derbe (Acts 13:14; Gal. 4:13–15; 2 Cor. 11:24–25; 2 Tim. 3:10–11). Apparently it was in another phase of Paul's missionary activity that the gospel was really planted in the territory of Asia, centering around Ephesus. This activity, which is reflected in Acts 18:19–21 and Acts 19:1 to 20:38, covered a period of approximately three years somewhere about A.D. 53–57. During this period of his ministry Paul divided his followers and sent them out into other areas of Asia Minor, with the result that geographically the gospel was introduced on a very extensive basis (Acts 19:10).

Ephesus was strategically located for the dissemination of the gospel to all of Asia Minor. The effectiveness of this ministry is reflected in the record of the book of Acts, where it is indicated that the people turned to Christianity in such great numbers that worship in the pagan religions so declined that the men who made a business of selling equipment for pagan worship brought an official complaint against the Christian leaders (Acts 19:23–41). The new religion was welcomed by great numbers of the people because of the prevailing condition of confusion where matters of religion were concerned and the failure of the religions of the day to bring satisfaction to the worshipers.

Long before this time Judaism had come to make its challenge in the Roman world. When the Jews were dispersed from Palestine and set up in colonies throughout the Roman Empire, they took their religion with them. Beyond this experience of dispersion, in the years that followed they traveled extensively, making their home in the cities of the Roman Empire, many of them with the privilege of Roman citizenship. Judaism was well known by the people of Asia Minor, and it offered to them its claim and its challenge at the point of religious devotion as they sought the good life. Judaism in Asia Minor had the same characteristics that it had in Palestine. It was distinctively a legalistic system in which one came to realize the good life by means of human attainment or merit. This human attainment or merit came about by strict observance of the Law and by strict observance of all the ceremonial rites which had come to be a part of religious practice. Salvation in Judaism was a matter of works, fully and completely. Christianity would challenge that position, asserting that salvation, or "the good life," was not a matter of human attainment but a matter of divine provision. Just as the teachings of Jesus had caused conflict between him and the leaders of the Jewish religion and just as Paul's preaching in Jerusalem had caused conflict between him and the leaders of the Jewish religion, so here, far removed from Jerusalem, Judaism and Christianity once again would engage in vital combat.

Greek philosophy, too, made its claim to the thought and life of the people of Asia Minor. For centuries the philosophers of the Greek culture had offered through their teaching the way of the good life as they understood it. To Greek philosophy it was not so much the matter of merit acquired through legal regulations as it was a state of release from the restraints of evil and a realization of personal peace and quiet achieved through intellectual processes, speculation, and rules of conduct. There were many different phases of Greek philosophy, but all of them pointed to this one end and all of them claimed the ability to lead the mind of man into such state of peace. Christianity would come into vital conflict with such a system because of its view that the good life—deliverance from evil, spiritual rest, peace, integration of personality—can come not by men's powers or processes but only by a power that is outside of man and which comes to indwell man in the person and presence of the living Christ. Such conflict between Christianity and Greek philosophy is found in the activity of the missionaries as recorded in the book of Acts, and it is reflected in several of the New Testament books.

Closely related to Greek philosophy, yet distinct from it, as a process and way to the good life was the claim and challenge of the mystery religions. These religions were known throughout the Roman world. Some of them had a background in Egypt, some in Persia, some in Greece, some in Roman life. While there were differences in names of the gods, in terminology, and in mythology, there were many striking points of parallel. These religions were, for the most part, cults stressing the processes of nature and fertility.

They were similar in that they had their temples, their priesthood, their priestesses, their worship forms and ceremonials all for the purpose of bringing to the individual the answer to his deep-felt spiritual needs and hungers. The particular worship at Ephesus was that of the goddess Diana, though other religious cults were well known there. One of the very strong rivals of Christianity for the loyalty and devotion of the people was the cult of Mithra. So strong was this movement that many New Testament scholars have felt that if the Roman world of the first four centuries had not gone Christian it would have become Mithraistic. These religions promised much, but they failed to produce for the individual the answer to his needs and the supply for his hunger.

Into this arena of religious and philosophical quests and confusion moved Christianity to offer its claims and challenge to the best of the mind and hearts of men. It will appear in the very opening verses of Ephesians that Christianity would be directly opposed to all these previously discussed views because of its basic position on the way to salvation or "the good life." Whereas these systems, both Jewish and Greek, held that salvation came by way of *human attainment*, Christianity held that it came completely by way of *divine provision*. Christianity held that man could not find his way to deliverance from evil and to salvation by his own efforts. He could find these only by what a benevolent God had provided through the redemptive work of his Son Jesus Christ.

That difference and conflict between Christianity and other religious systems so long ago still stands as a basic approach to life and to destiny. Many years ago a Jewish rabbi lectured our class in New Testament three days on the basic doctrine and practices of the Jewish faith. The fourth day was given over to a forum in which the students were permitted to ask the rabbi any questions relative to his religion and his view of Christianity. One of the questions was this: "What as you see it is the basic difference between your religion (that of the Old Testament) and our religion (that of the New Testament)?" Without hesitating, but with remarkable discernment, the rabbi answered: "My religion is a religion of the hands, doing the works of the law as a means of being right with God. Your religion is a religion of the heart, believing that someone else (that is, Jesus Christ) has done for you what you could never do for yourself to make you right with God." No more exact distinction than that can be found. That is precisely the difference when one comes to the last analysis, and it was that precise difference which brought Christianity into conflict with other religious systems from its very beginning. With that distinction in mind we look at basic Christianity as it is reflected in the epistle to the Ephesians.

I

The Plan of Redemption

1:1 to 2:10

In a consideration of basic Christianity the starting point must be with the plan of redemption which is set out in this religious system. Nothing can be more basic than that; without it there could be no Christianity. This theme occupies the opening discussion in the Ephesian epistle. It is introduced even in the brief salutation found in verses 1–2. Paul speaks of himself as *an apostle of Christ Jesus through the will of God.* The word "apostle" was built on a Greek verb meaning "to send with a message." The apostles of the Christian religion were those whom Christ sent as the bearers of the good news of redemption that God was in Christ reconciling men to himself. Paul was not one of that original twelve which Jesus sent forth. He regarded himself as an apostle, however, in just as genuine a sense as the twelve. He, too, was commissioned of Christ, and his commission was to take the gospel to the Gentile world. This apostleship was extended through the will of God. The word "will" is a translation of a Greek word which, in its origin, stemmed from the verb meaning "to wish." It was the wish of God that Paul should be sent by Christ as a bearer of the good news of redemption.

Paul addresses his letter to *the saints who are in Ephesus and the faithful ones in Christ Jesus.* The word "saint" means literally "holy ones." In its New Testament usage it did not mean what it is sometimes construed to mean today. It did not mean a dead person who by virtue of his life had been canonized so that he was a person who could be addressed in prayer. Nor did it mean one who was without sin. It was a word describing persons who because of their relationship to Christ had been set apart from the people of the world as a people who belonged peculiarly to God. It means about what the word "Christian" means today when it is used in its proper sense and not in the very general or loose sense which covers anyone who might claim to be a part of the Christian religion.

In previous discussion it has been noted that the expression "in Ephesus" does not appear in the best Greek manuscripts of Ephesians. The reasons for its absence have been mentioned in brief manner, with the probable solution to the problem being the circular nature of this letter; the name of the particular church where the letter was being read would be inserted at this point in the public reading. The expression "the faithful ones in Christ Jesus" is a synonym for the saints. While the word "saint" is an adjective meaning "holy," the word "faithful" is an adjective meaning "believing." The message is addressed then to those who are identified as being the people of Christ, set apart and believing in him.

The theme of redemption is further introduced in this salutation by the prayer in verse 2, *Grace to you and peace from God our Father and the Lord Jesus Christ.* This prayer is found in all of the letters of Paul. In the pastoral epistles a third word is included, being inserted in this form, "Grace, mercy, and peace." [1] The words "grace" and "peace" are most

[1] 1 Tim. 1:2; 2 Tim. 1:2, and some manuscripts of Titus 1:4.

significant. Grace is the unmerited favor which God bestows upon man in relationship to the redemptive work of Christ. Peace is the condition which results in the heart of man when grace has done its work. Sin and conscience, like twin hunters, hound man in his life and his attempt to do what is right. Grace and peace defeat these hunters. Grace takes care of the problem of sin; peace takes care of the problem of conscience. They stand in proper sequence. Just as in the Old Testament sacrificial system the sin offerings had to precede the peace offering, so here grace must do its work before there can be any peace in the heart of man. Paul's combination of grace (a Greek concept) and peace (a Hebrew concept) makes for a most forceful prayer for the very highest blessing to every believer. This grace and peace have their source in God the Father and the Lord Jesus Christ. Apart from what God has done in Christ there could be neither grace nor peace for man. With this grand introduction, Paul approaches the most basic idea in the Christian religion.

The Provision of Redemption, 1:1–14

Nowhere in the New Testament will one find a more exalted passage than this one long sentence which extends through verses 3–14. Well has it been called "Paul's Hymn of Praise to the Redemptive Work of the Trinity."[2] Without discussing this unusual Christian concept of God as three-in-one, Paul shows the work of all three in providing redemption. There are three stanzas in this hymn, and each is followed by the same chorus. This will be observed in the

[2] Charles R. Erdman, *The Epistle of Paul to the Ephesians* (Philadelphia: The Westminster Press, 1931), p. 27. A similar term, "Paul's Chant of Thanksgiving," is used by Edgar Young Mullins, *Studies in Ephesians and Colossians* (Nashville: The Sunday School Board of the Southern Baptist Convention, 1913), p. 20.

more detailed discussion of the paragraph. The three stanzas relate to the work of the Father, of the Son, and of the Spirit. The chorus which follows each stanza indicates that this work was done to the praise of the glorious grace of God. Remember, as previously indicated, that Paul presents this idea of the divine provision of redemption against the background of the standard Judaism and the standard Greek philosophy of the day, both of which looked upon the matter of salvation, deliverance from evil, the good life as a matter of human attainment. Paul's insistence is that it is not a matter of human merit or achievement. It is a divine gift which God has worked out in Christ and which he offers to man on the basis of faith.

The Work of the Father, 1:3–6

The presentation of the provision of redemption starts appropriately with the work of the Father God. The entire passage is a doxology in form, an expression of praise to God for his redemptive work. He appears in this passage as elsewhere as a God of purpose, of grace, and of glory. Verse 3 exclaims, *Blessed (be) the God and Father of our Lord Jesus Christ, who has blessed us with every spiritual blessing in the heavenlies in Christ.* The adjective "blessed" means "to be praised" or "worthy of praise." God is thus described in his intrinsic character as one who is worthy of man's praise. In the New Testament this word is used only of God, never of man or any other creature.

In doxologies like this the verb is most often unexpressed and is to be supplied by the reader. That is true in this instance. The English translation "be" is inserted, though not a part of the original text. Interpreters differ as to what form of the verb should be inserted. Some understand the need of an imperative—"let be"; some, an optative—"Oh, that he might be"; some, a simple indicative—"Blessed is the God and Father." That is not a matter of supreme importance. It is a matter of supreme importance that this word referring to God's worthiness or praise is given the most emphatic position in the sentence—first place. It is the God of Christian revelation, the Father of our Lord Jesus Christ, who is thus praised.

He is praised because he has "blessed us with every spiritual blessing." In the abundance of his mercy he has poured out upon man every spiritual blessing which man is capable of receiving. God is often recognized as the giver of material blessings. Here, however, the emphasis is on more important things—spiritual blessings. Every spiritual blessing which man has is from God. Every spiritual blessing which man is capable of receiving God gives. All of this activity has been carried out "in the heavenlies." This is a word which appears five times in the epistle. In this instance it emphasizes the realm in which this spiritual blessing is carried out. It is the divine realm of activity altogether. It is not an activity which is related to the human realm; it is one which is limited to the divine. It is "in the highest heavenly places" that God has worked out his redemptive purpose for man.

The realm of this activity is further defined by the expression "in Christ." Every spiritual blessing which God has bestowed upon us has been in Christ. The term "in Christ" is one of Paul's favorite expressions for Christian relationship. As a term for organizing the theology of Paul, this is perhaps superior to every other term that he uses. More of his thinking can be placed under this expression "in Christ" than any other one term. The phrase must certainly refer to all the redemptive work of Christ in the experience of his incarnation, his death, his resurrection, his ascension, his heavenly priesthood, his eternal purpose for man. All that has been done by way of spiritual blessing has been done for us "in Christ." [3]

Verse 4, *just as he chose us in him before the foundation of the world, in order that we might be holy and blameless before him in love.* This verse constitutes what is known as a modal clause. It tells *how* the previous activity was carried out. It was carried out by means of God's elective choice. From the word translated "he chose" we derive our word "election." God has blessed us with every spiritual blessing by means of his elective choice.

We do not understand, of course, exactly what this involves. It does not mean, as some have assumed, that God saves or condemns men in violation of their own wills. Nor should it cause disturbance in one's mind by raising the question about those who are outside of the Christian religion, that is, "Were they not chosen of God?" Paul's emphasis here is not on those who are not Christians. It is an expression of praise to God for what he has done for those who *are* Christians.

It must be recognized that God is a free Being. He chooses on the basis of his sovereignty and his absolute foreknowledge of the total individual. The New Testament truth is that all have sinned and all deserve condemnation. The fact that God "elects" some to salvation is not an indication of injustice where others are concerned; it is an indication of grace where anyone is concerned. We may not know why God worked in some particular way. We can know that in his infinite knowledge and good will he knew that that was the best way and he moved in that way. The purpose of this text is magnifying the fact that an infinite God has moved into the area of the experience of finite man to pour out

[3] Note the use of "in Christ" or "in him" in this paragraph: vv. 3, 6–7, 9–13.

spiritual blessings upon him in relationship to the redemptive work of Christ.

This was no afterthought on the part of God. It was a reality "before the foundation of the world." The word "foundation" is the most basic word that could be used in such an expression. Literally it means "before the throwing down of the world." Before the foundation on which the world was to be built was laid, God had his redemptive purpose in mind. As in Romans 8:28–30 God's work here is described as reaching from eternity to eternity.

A matter too often overlooked is that of the purpose of God's choice and blessings as it is set out here in verse 4, "that we might be holy and blameless before him in love." God has blessed us in Christ as he has chosen us in Christ, and the end of that choice is a cleansed believer or worshiper. In the New Testament the doctrine of election is not a dry theological bone at which people gnaw. It is, rather, a living, vital doctrine which man sees in operation every day of his experience. The end of that elective choice is an individual cleansed of his sin, remade in the spiritual likeness of God, and, hence, a fit object for God's fellowship. This holiness and spotlessness is further described by the expression "before him." It is not a holiness and spotlessness in the eyes of men. Men are too much inclined to accept lower standards and that which would not be spotless. It is holiness and blamelessness in the presence of Christ himself. God has chosen us to be people of this character even in the eyes of Christ.

The term "in love" is variously interpreted. Some interpreters relate it to this holiness and spotlessness, indicating the large general area of Christian life in which this holiness and spotlessness is realized. God has chosen us that we should be holy and blameless before him in the large area of

Christian love—love for God and love for our fellow man. This may be the correct interpretation. Many interpreters, however, see the expression as having more meaning if it is related to that which follows, as an indication of the area in which God's work of foreordination was carried out. For that reason for present purposes it is included both in the fourth and in the fifth verses, that the reader may see both ideas and may weigh the evidences to his own satisfaction.

Verse 5, *in love having foreordained us into sonship through Jesus Christ unto himself according to the good pleasure of his will.* This verse continues the idea of the work of the Father in providing redemption for sinful man. It is in direct sequence to the verbs which have preceded it. God has blessed us just as he chose us, in love having foreordained us. The three cannot be separated. They all relate to the same divine activity. Love shows the area in which this work of foreordination took place. What does God the Father do in providing redemption for man? He loves us; he chooses us; he foreordains us. Some interpreters see in the expression "having foreordained" only a temporal idea. If we transliterate the word into English, it says, "He before-horizoned us," that is, he drew a circle about us. This would be in line with the expression "before the foundation of the world." He drew a circle about us before the foundation of the world. Because of the meaning of the two words most of the interpreters do not understand "foreordained" to have a temporal force only but rather also to have a modal force telling *how* God chose. He chose by foreordaining. He chose by "before-horizoning," drawing a circle about us. Surely the doctrine of foreordination and the doctrine of election in the New Testament are, to all practical purposes, identical.

God foreordained us, or marked us off, unto sonship. This word might more properly be translated "unto adoption as sons." It was a word with a background of Roman practice[4] which meant to take one from outside the family, to bring him in, and to give him family standing. So Paul sees God's work in providing redemption as a work which takes those who were alien to him, brings them in, and makes them sons of God. This is done "through Jesus Christ" and it is done "unto himself," that is, unto God himself. Through Christ God brings to himself aliens and gives them standing as sons. Further, it was done according to the good pleasure of his will. The expression "good pleasure" means that which seemed good. That which seemed good according to his will or his wish he has done in making aliens to be sons of God.

The chorus which follows in verse 6 indicates that all of this was *to the praise of the glory of his grace, which he freely poured out upon us in the Beloved One*. All that God has done in providing redemption for sinful man has been done to the praise of his glorious grace. As grateful recipients of God's redemptive work, it is natural that we should think first of the benefit that comes to us as we experience this grace. In the New Testament, however, the major emphasis is not on the benefit that comes to the individual who receives this grace. It is rather on the benefit that accrues to God who has extended this grace. Ultimately all that he does in redemption returns to speak with praise of the glorious favor which he bestows upon unworthy and sinful men. It is a tribute to his righteous character which is redemptive in nature that he will not see man in his sin and do nothing about it. He moves into the experience of man redemptively to make a creature of fit character to have fellowship with God.

---

[4] For the possible Jewish background for the practice, see William H. Rossell, "New Testament Adoption—Graeco-Roman or Semitic?" *Journal of Biblical Literature*, LXXI (December, 1952), 233–34.

This glorious grace he has freely or lavishly poured out upon us in the Beloved One. This expression "Beloved One" is a perfect passive participle built on the strongest Greek word for love. It is used here as a title for the redeeming Christ. He is the Beloved One of the Father, and it is in him and in relationship to him that we come to be recipients of God's grace.

The Work of the Son, 1:7–12

The use of the term "the Beloved One" introduces the work of the Second Person of the Trinity, that is, the Son of God, in providing redemption for man. The discussion begins with a relative pronoun to indicate further our participation in this plan of redemption in relationship to Jesus Christ.

Verse 7, *in whom we have our redemption through his blood, that is, the forgiveness of our trespasses, according to the riches of his grace.* It is in Christ that we have redemption. The tense of the verb "have" speaks of the present reality of the possession. Redemption is ours as a present possession. This is the conception found throughout the New Testament. It is not to deny that there is a sense in which the future will reveal many things relative to our redemption. It is, however, a strong expression of confidence that redemption is ours as a possession of present reality. Attention should be given to the presence of the definite article with the noun "redemption." We have "the redemption." The use of the definite article points out the particular redemption experienced by every Christian, long looked for by the Jews, now an accomplished fact and experienced, as will be indicated later, by Jew and Gentile alike. Besides indicating particular identity, the definite article in Greek sometimes is used with the force of a personal pronoun. It is so understood here by many interpreters, hence the translation "our redemption." Although there is no personal pronoun in the text, the translation is entirely legitimate because of this usage.

The word "redemption" means a release or a deliverance effected by payment of a price. It was a market term familiar to every reader of the epistle. This idea of the payment of a price or a ransom has sometimes in the history of Christian interpretation been stretched to cover unfortunate explanations which do not seem to be a part of the New Testament approach to the doctrine of redemption. Some have interpreted it to mean that God had to pay Satan a ransom price in order to redeem men and the ransom price was the blood of Christ. Some have looked upon it as though God were paying himself that which was due his infinite person by way of a ransom price and that ransom price was the blood of Christ. Such interpretations appear to go beyond what is meant by this word in the New Testament. Apparently it means only deliverance. From the penalty and the bondage of sin we have been delivered by the redemptive work of God in Christ.

This deliverance was accomplished at the cost of the death of Christ on the cross. If one would know what it cost God to forgive sin, he must look at the cross and see what sin did to the One that God loved. It is not easy to forgive; it is not easy to forgive one who has hurt you personally; it is even harder to forgive one who has hurt someone that you love. The cross of Christ stands as the most graphic representation of what it cost God to deliver man from his sin. The expression "through his blood" is the direct reference to the cross. His was not an ordinary death. It was death as a sacrifice. Christ so interpreted his death in the institution of the Lord's Supper (Matt. 26:28; Mark 14:24). He interpreted his death on the cross, that is, his blood, as a means of the ratification of a new covenant relationship between God and man. So in the New Testament the blood of Christ has the sense of the effective power of his death in the purification of the sinner in the victory over sin itself. It is the means of removing from man that sin and guilt which constituted a barrier between him and God, with the result that fellowship with God is made possible for man.

This redemption through the sacrificial work of Christ consists of the forgiveness of our trespasses. The word translated "forgiveness" means literally "the sending away of our trespasses." It was used in many ways by the Greek people. It was used of the release of water from a reservoir so that it was sent away. It was used of horses in a race in the sense that they were sent away from the post. It was used of prisoners at the bar as they were dismissed or pardoned, released from the penalty of their evil deed. It is in relationship to the death of Christ on the cross that our sins may be dismissed, sent away from us. The particular reference here is to personal acts of sin. The translation "trespass" indicates that this is very close to the word "transgress," though there is a different Greek word for the latter. The word translated "trespass" looks upon sin as a misdeed or a lapse from proper conduct. It appears always to view sin as an act rather than as a condition or a power as we find it in the word which is usually translated "sin." Again the definite article appears to be used with the force of a personal pronoun. The trespasses in reality are "our trespasses." In the redemption which Christ brings about we experience the sending away of our personal acts of sin against God.

This forgiveness of our trespasses is "according to the riches of his grace." The term translated "according to" is a term which relates to the idea of the old algebraic formula of proportions: $x:y::1:2$ (x is to y as 1 is to 2). Paul's meaning is that we have the forgiveness of trespasses in proportion to the riches of God's grace. Our forgiveness is not in proportion to our merit. It is not in proportion to a price which we might pay or a work which we might do. It is in direct proportion to the riches or the abundance of the grace of God. Paul, as a former Pharisee who had tried so very hard to live up to the requirements of the law only to experience frustration, had the highest possible appreciation for God's grace, God's unmerited favor given to man in the work of Christ. This word "grace" has a large place in all of Paul's epistles. It is the very nerve center of his teaching concerning the redemption of sinful man. In its general usage it sometimes meant "beauty" in contrast to "ugliness," "order" in contrast to "disorder," "free gift" in contrast to "merit." Everywhere in Paul's writing it involves the idea of the free gift of God, the undeserved merit which God grants to man. It speaks of the very nature of God, who delights to give to the object of his love that which is needed. So here forgiveness of personal trespasses is in proportion to the wealth or the riches of the unmerited favor which God extends.

Verses 8–9, *which* (*grace*) *he has abounded to us in all wisdom and understanding, making known to us the mystery of his will, according to his good pleasure which he purposed in him.*

The idea in the word "abound" is that of supplying so richly that there is not just enough but more than enough. It goes beyond the bare necessity. God has extended to us unmerited favor sufficient to send away all our personal trespasses and to go far beyond that in its effectiveness. It covers the entire life and activity of the individual in his relationship to requirement and to God. To us God has abundantly supplied this grace in the area of "wisdom and understanding." The two nouns doubtless are close synonyms. There is, however, a basic difference. The word translated "wisdom" means the ability to make the right choice when faced with multiple choice. It is the kind of wisdom which James says that God will give liberally to the one who needs it and who will petition for it (James 1:5). The word translated "understanding" or "prudence" speaks specifically of the area of intelligent action. In the Greek translation of the Old Testament it was used of the wisdom which God gave to Solomon. The joining of the two words in this text apparently presents the idea of total or complete wisdom. This grace of God has been extended to us in the area of moral intelligence or insight and in the area of the practical expression of wisdom.

Verse 9 indicates that this extension of grace in the area of wisdom and understanding was realized in God's revealing to us, i.e., to Christians generally, the mystery of his will according to his good pleasure which he purposed in Christ. In Greek usage the word "mystery" spoke of that which was secret and which could be known only by way of revelation. In Paul's use of the term he means that that which once was hidden has now been revealed of God and is a secret made open. It applies in this sense to God's work of redemption in its entirety (Eph. 6:19; Col. 1:26; Rom. 16:25; 1 Cor. 2:7; 1 Tim. 3:9, 16), as well as applying in other instances to particular phases of God's plan, such as his including the Gentiles in this plan of redemption (Eph. 3:3–9; Rom. 11:25), the transforming of Christians who live at the time of the Lord's Second Coming (1 Cor. 15:52), and Christ's union with the body of which he is the head (Eph. 5:32). "Mystery," then, means that which could not be explained and understood until in the purpose of God it was brought out into the open by way of divine revelation. Such is the nature of the grace which God extends to sinful men. No man could ever on his own initiative work out such a plan.

Man naturally is inclined to the idea that he can be right with God only by means of some works which he must do. It is a matter of divine revelation that man can be right with God by means of unmerited favor which god bestows through the redemptive work of Christ.

All of this revelation of the mystery of his will was "according to his good pleasure which he purposed in him." It was the good pleasure of God to give this grace, and the good pleasure of giving was a part of God's purpose with reference to the redemptive work of Christ. Some interpreters understand the expression "in him" to have a reflexive force which would mean that this was done according to God's purpose "in himself." If this is correct, it would mean that this was a part of the self-purpose expression of God. Most of the interpreters, however, feel that the term is a reference to Christ. There is good evidence for that in the light of the fact that these terms "in Christ," "in him," "in whom," and "in the Beloved One" are used with such freedom in this paragraph. It is certainly God's own free determination which is expressed in this grace, but it is a determination which is expressed in relationship to Christ and his redemptive mission.

This which God has purposed is further set out in verse 10, *unto a dispensation of the fulness of the times, to head up all things in Christ, the things in the heavens and the things on the earth.* The word translated "dispensation" means also stewardship. Here is seen the end of all of that which God purposed in his redemptive work in Christ. The preposition translated "unto" appears to mean "with reference to" and hence to stress further the design of God in Christ's work. According to the New Testament it was in the fulness of time that Christ came to do his work; that is, it was not until the world was ready for such that his work could be carried out. The word "dispensation" appears to have the sense of administration. All the universe, man included, is looked upon as a great household of God or body of God's possessions. This is an administration which is related to the fulness of time or to the fitness of time. The meaning is that it was the purpose of God that when the time was right for it Christ would come in his work of administration of the things of God; this work was basically redemptive. When he came, all previous administrations were finished in the sense that they reached their climax in him.

God's purpose in this administration or stewardship of Christ's redemptive work extends beyond the fact of the cross. It extends on to the ultimate purpose of God in the absolute sense. This is observed in the expression "to sum up all things in Christ." This is an infinitive of a verb which was used in military affairs to describe the way a regiment which had been scattered in battle in conflict with the enemy would be gathered up under the leadership of their captain. Paul seems to picture all the household things of God's possession as having been scattered in the conflict with the forces of evil. It was his purpose that he would gather up all these scattered holdings and put them under one supreme captain, Jesus Christ. The absolute nature of this purpose is seen when Paul says that this refers to heavenly things and to earthly things. Christ deserves to be the one head or the one captain of all the possessions of the eternal God, and it was God's purpose that in relationship to his redemptive work that would become reality. In the purpose of God it *has become* reality now, and the New Testament bids Christians look to the future when we shall *see* the reality of the complete victory of Christ over every enemy, the last of which will be death itself (1 Cor. 15:54).

Verse 11, *in whom we were made an inheritance also, hav-*

ing been foreordained according to the purpose of the One who works all things according to the counsel of his will. Here Paul indicates that we have come to be a part of God's inheritance through this work of Christ and his coming to be the captain or administrator of all of God's affairs. This too was no afterthought on the part of God. We had been foreordained (before-horizoned) as an inheritance for God according to the purpose of God himself. The word "purpose" means literally "that which is set before one." God set it before himself that we should be his heritage in relationship to the redemptive work of Christ. This was all done by the one "who works all things according to the counsel of his will." Everything that God does is in line with the counsel of his will. Here in striking connection are the two basic New Testament words relating to the will of God—counsel and will. The first one carries the idea of a plan; the second carries the idea of wish. What does God plan; what does God wish? Certainly, in the ultimate sense they come to mean one and the same, but the emphasis here is that all of this work has been done by One who does everything according to the plan which he wills to carry out.

Verse 12 brings at the close of this second stanza the same general chorus which came at the close of the first stanza, *to the end that we should be unto the praise of his glory, those who had before-hoped in Christ.* The term "those who had before-hoped in Christ" apparently is a reference to Jewish people who found their messianic expectations fulfilled in Christ. They had hoped in him, and now, having come to know him in his redemptive work, they themselves come to be the means of expressing praise to the glory of God. What Christ did in his work of giving his own blood to secure forgiveness of sin was ultimately to the praise of the glory of God. It is to the praise of the glory of God that many of the Jewish people who had before hoped in the Messiah recognized him in Christ and as a result followed him.

The Work of the Holy Spirit, 1:13–14

Beginning in verse 13 Paul makes a transition in two ways. One transition is seen in his moving from the work of Christ to the work of the Holy Spirit in providing redemption. This is the third stanza in the hymn of praise, and it will be followed by a chorus as were the other stanzas. Another transition in verse 13 appears to be from attention to the Jews and their relationship to the gospel to the Gentiles and their relationship to the gospel. Verse 13, *in whom you also having heard the word of truth, the gospel of your salvation, in whom having believed also, you were sealed by the Holy Spirit of promise.* The personal pronoun "you" seems to be in contrast to the personal pronoun "we" in verse 12. "We who had before-hoped in Christ" seems to refer to the Jews; "you also" seems to refer to the Gentiles. The Jews who had before-hoped in Christ have found in him a Redeemer. The Gentiles, also, who heard the gospel of salvation and responded by faith found in Christ a Redeemer.

The word "gospel" means literally "the good news." The good news of salvation was that in Christ God provided redemption for man apart from human attainment or achievement in any way and on the basis of his unmerited favor toward man. The Gentiles needed such a message as did the Jews, and they received that message through the witness borne to them through gospel preaching. They heard the word of truth. They believed the one about whom that word spoke. The faith which brings redemption is faith in a divine Person. That person is Jesus Christ, the Son of God. When they had heard the word and when they had believed Christ about whom the word spoke, they were sealed by the promised Holy Spirit.

The Holy Spirit, who had been promised by Jesus in the days of his earthly ministry, came at Pentecost to harvest the seed which had been planted by Jesus. This was most appropriate in that Pentecost was the harvest thanksgiving festival in the religious life of the Jewish people. Christ in the days of his flesh planted the seed. In his redemptive work the Holy Spirit came at Pentecost as the great harvester. It is the Holy Spirit who seals the believer.

The interpreters differ in their approach to the grammatical construction found in the term "the Holy Spirit." Some look upon it as locative, emphasizing the area or location within which the believer is sealed. This would mean that the believer is sealed "in the Holy Spirit," the metaphor being that of a container into which an object is placed and within which the object is sealed. It is possible that that is the significance of the construction. There is just as good evidence, however, that in this instance the grammatical construction is the instrumental case, telling by whom the believer is sealed. The word translated "seal" was the word for putting upon an object an identifying and possessive mark. It was used of a mark that was for the purpose of confirming, securing, authenticating, or marking for particular possession. In this instance it is God's possessive and securing seal placed upon the believer. Hearing and believing come in proper sequence, and when one has heard and has believed, the Holy Spirit puts God's seal, God's branding iron, upon the individual to say, "This one belongs to me for time and for eternity."

Verse 14, *who is an earnest of our inheritance, looking to the redemption of God's cherished possession, unto the praise of his glory*. The Holy Spirit is looked upon here as an "earnest" of our inheritance. This was a commercial term used for money paid down in pledge that the full contract would be carried out in due time. The Holy Spirit is for the believer God's guarantee that his full contract to give the believer an eternal inheritance will be carried out in due time. The believer's present possession of the Holy Spirit is but a partial payment of all that redemption ultimately will mean for him. This partial payment is the same in kind as the complete possession to be realized later. All that God does for us in the Holy Spirit is but a foretaste of all that he purposes to do in due time. This partial payment is a guarantee from God that the full possession of the inheritance will one day be realized by the believer. The Holy Spirit serves as such an earnest, "looking forward to the redemption of God's peculiar possession." This is a rather exact translation of the construction which speaks of the forward look in the Christian religion. This forward look implies a past experience; it implies a present condition; it implies a future state in which salvation is to be consummated as the believer comes into the full inheritance which is his as a son of God. Elsewhere in the New Testament, that is related to the resurrection of the body and the believer's entering upon his eternal home with Christ. This work of the Holy Spirit is followed by the same chorus, "unto the praise of his glory." It is to the praise of the glorious grace of God that Father, Son, and Spirit have worked and continue to work redemptively in the experience of men.

The Blessings of Redemption, 1:15 to 2:10

The one supreme fact relative to the matter of redemption is that God has provided this redemption for sinful man. Next in order of importance is the fact of the blessings that come to man when he experiences this redemption. These blessings

Paul discusses, beginning in Ephesians 1:15. This is a section that is typical of Paul; in it he combines his discussion of the matter at hand with an expression of thanksgiving for those who are the recipients of the letter. Similar expressions of thanksgiving are found in Romans 1:8, 1 Corinthians 1:4, 2 Thessalonians 1:3, Philippians 1:3, Colossians 1:3, and Philemon 4. This speaks of a gracious spirit and habit of expressing thanksgiving for those to whom he writes. He has heard of their faith in the Lord. He has heard of their love as expressed toward all believers, and he thanks God continuously for them. The expression in verse 16, "cease not to give thanks," means rather exactly, "I let nothing stop me from giving thanks." He wants the readers to know of his thanksgiving for their Christian standing, and he wants them to appreciate fully what redemption in Christ can really mean and what it can really accomplish in human experience.

A Clear Insight into the Nature of Redemption, 1:15–19

This expression of thanksgiving and prayer introduces the first of the blessings of redemption. Verse 17 gives an introduction to the content of Paul's prayer, *that the God of our Lord Jesus Christ, the Father of glory, may give to you a spirit of wisdom and revelation in full knowledge of him.* The prayer is that the readers may be given of God the ability to know fully all the blessings that are theirs in Christ. They can have this full knowledge only through divinely imparted wisdom and revelation. The full blessings of Christ are such that they can be appreciated only as the hand of God lifts the veil to reveal them to men.

Verses 18–19, *having the eyes of your heart enlightened in order that you may understand what is the hope of his calling, what is the wealth of the glory of his inheritance among the saints, and what is the abounding greatness of his power with reference to us who are believing, according to the working of the strength of his sufficiency.* With this spirit of wisdom and revelation in full knowledge of Christ, the believers will have their spiritual eyes opened. The term "the eyes of your heart" seems to be a metaphorical reference to spiritual sight. With their spiritual eyes open they will have clear insight into the nature of redemption. This clear insight will be realized in three particular ways. First, they will understand the hope of Christ's calling. All of the Christian religion is related to the element of hope. All of it is related to the factor of the call which Christ has extended to men. Christian hope is placed in that call. When one has his spiritual eyes open, he knows as he never knew before just what is involved in the eternal hope which is in the heart of one who has responded to Christ's call to salvation and to service.

Second, by spiritually enlightened eyes one sees "the wealth of the glory of his inheritance in the saints." The pronoun "his" in this expression apparently refers to God. The entire expression is a tribute to the fact that believers come to be God's inheritance, but, more than that, they come to experience an inheritance which is gloriously rich in its every connotation. God has invested much in the saints, that is, in the believers. All of this results in a rich inheritance for him and for them.

Third, spiritually enlightened eyes have clear insight for understanding "the abounding greatness of his power with reference to us who believe." This is an expression of power which cannot be known apart from the matter of divine revelation. This is a day of the demonstration of power such as Paul and his contemporaries could never know. When man would demonstrate his power, he builds a plane that can outstrip sound in its speed; he sends a man-made satellite into orbit, whirling around the earth at unbelievable speed; he releases the energy that for countless years has been latent in the atoms of a piece of uranium and builds a bomb that can destroy millions of lives in a matter of seconds. None of this, however, can approach the exceeding greatness of God's power. When God would demonstrate his power, he releases his Spirit in the heart of one who believes in him, and by so doing he makes a good man out of a bad man; he makes a good man in a bad world. No power which man can generate or release is able to do that. One must experience redemption and have eyes that are spiritually open in order to appreciate fully the greatness of this power of God in those who believe. It is power which is "according to the working of the strength of his sufficiency." Here again is the algebraic construction relative to proportion. The power that he works in one who believes is in proportion to the powerful energy of God's sufficiency. Here are three nouns which are similar in their significance, and yet they vary a bit in their basic meaning—power, strength, sufficiency. All of them must be combined with the word "working" or "energy." This is the nature of what man has experienced in redemption. These are the spiritual riches which are his in Christ.

A Full Insight into the Nature of Christ, 1:20–23

Another of the blessings of redemption is realized in the fact that only the redeemed can fully comprehend and appreciate the nature of Christ. This is directly related to the preceding passage, as it is introduced by an indication that the same kind of power which God releases in the believer is the power by which he raised Christ from the dead. Verse 20, *which he worked in Christ, when he raised him from the dead, and seated him at his right hand in the heavenlies.*

A full comprehension of the nature of Christ grasps the truth of his resurrection from the dead. This is a fact which has a most prominent place in the New Testament. Jesus Christ did not experience the decay and decomposition which other bodies experience when buried. His body was raised from the dead and so transformed and glorified that it could never again be subject to the limitations which it had known, and it can never again experience death. The cross is at all times central in the New Testament message of redemption, but to those early writers and preachers the cross would have had little meaning apart from the resurrection of Christ. Man cannot scoff and mock at sin and death as he looks at the cross. It is only when he comes to the empty tomb and the truth of the resurrection of Christ that he can scoff at sin and death and say, "Thanks be to God who gives us the victory." No concept of Christ can be the New Testament concept if it stops short of the resurrection.

A second thing about Christ which is understood more fully by the redeemed has to do with his exaltation. Having been raised from the dead, he has taken his seat in the position of honor and authority in the heavenlies, supremely exalted above every kind of rule or ruler and supremely exalted above every name that might be related to authority and power in the present age as well as in future ages. This statement is embraced in the closing part of verse 20 and in all of verse 21. It does not stand alone in the New Testament as an expression of the exalted position of the ascended Christ. The writer of the epistle to the Hebrews stated the fact most graphically in saying that when the Son of God had completed his redemptive work of making cleansing for sin he sat down at the right hand of Majesty in the heights (Heb. 1:3–4). This indicates a work satisfactorily completed and a reign victoriously started. It looks backward in approval of the work done in redemption; it looks forward to the result of that work in the lordship of Christ in human affairs in the present age and eternally.

A third phase of the nature of Christ which is seen fully only by the redeemed is expressed in verse 22, *he put all things in subjection under his feet, and gave him to be head over all things in the church.* This is an extension of the idea of the authority of Christ growing out of the completion of the earthly phase of his redemptive work through his death and resurrection. He ascended to the place of authority and power in heaven, having everything subjected to him. The "all things" which are subjected to him must be understood only in the comprehensive sense. Though there is still in the world opposition to the power and authority of Christ, in the purpose of God everything has been subjected to him and is as really subjected to him as though it were historically an accomplished fact.

Included in this subjecting of everything to him is the idea of his being made head over all things in the church. The church in verse 23 is identified as his body, the fulness of the One who fills all things in all men. This latter expression is one which almost defies understanding or explanation. Certainly included in it is the fact that the spiritual body made up of the redeemed has one head and one only, and that is the living Christ. If in the writings of Paul there is a sense in which the term "church" refers to all true believers everywhere, it is in this Ephesian letter. While the term "church" predominately in the New Testament refers to a local body of people who have been called out redemptively by Christ, it is most difficult to escape the impression that in this letter Paul ideally is enlarging the significance of the word to make it embrace all true believers. These make up the spiritual body of which Christ is the head; they fill out the remainder of the body. All together believers and Christ make one great spiritual body. This is a favorite illustration of Paul and will be found more fully discussed in Ephesians 4.

This redemption in Christ is tremendous in scope, but only those who have experienced the redemption can have the fullest insight into its nature and significance. There is but one Lord; there can be only one, and that is Christ. There is but one way of redemption; there can be only one, and that is provided through Christ. To grasp this is to know the genuine blessings offered in redemption.

A Transition from Death to Life, 2:1–9

Another of the blessings of redemption in Christ is the believer's transition from the darkness of the gloom of spiritual death to the glorious light of spiritual life. This is perhaps the first blessing as one ordinarily approaches the matter. It is natural that one who has experienced this redemption in Christ should think first in terms of the reality of salvation, that is, of spiritual life which is his in Christ. Paul would not minimize this blessing, even though in his discussion he speaks first of one's insight into the nature of redemption and one's insight into the nature of Christ. This paragraph is presented by means of the strongest possible contrast between "once" and "now." The spiritual condition of man *before* he came to participate in this redemption is given in contrast to his spiritual condition *after* he has come to be the recipient of this redemption.

Verse 1, *And you being dead in your trespasses and sins* (*he made alive*). The pronoun "you" refers to all who have come to experience redemption. Once they were dead in trespasses and sins. Death is frequently used in the New Testament in a metaphorical sense. It is used of the eternal destiny of the wicked in the sense that it is "a second death," in that they are cut off forever from any blessing or fellowship with God. It is used of living men who are unbelievers in the sense that they are inactive where God is concerned and they are dead in contrast to the condition of believers which is described as life. It is in this spiritual sense that the word is used here. The words "trespasses and sins" seem to speak of the area in which this death is experienced rather than the means by which it was experienced. They are dead in the realm of trespasses and sins. This is the more impressive when one looks into verse 10 and sees the fact stated that God's purpose is that man should walk about in the realm of good works. It is a contrast between being dead in the area of trespasses and sins and being alive and walking about in the area of good works. The word for trespasses is the same one which appeared in Ephesians 1:7, personal acts of evil. The word translated "sins" is the more general word, which relates to sin as a habit or sin as a power.

Verse 2, *in which once you walked about according to the worldly fashion of the age, according to the ruler of the authority of the air, the spirit now working in the sons of disobedience.* Note again the contrast with verse 10. God's purpose for these believers was that they should walk about in good works, but they were engaged in walking about in trespasses and in sins instead. This speaks, of course, of their condition before they came within the scope of the redemptive work of Christ. The term "according to the worldly fashion of the day" is an attempt to translate an expression which literally translated would be "according to the age of this world." The former translation appears to get closer to what Paul has in mind. It means about what a person means today when he refers to "the spirit of the times." It has to do with a way of life which is in conformity with that which is fashionable from the viewpoint of the world. The German people have a term which for a one-word expression is superior to anything we have in English, *Zeitgeist*. This means rather literally "time spirit." There was a time when these readers had lived according to such pattern.

Their way of life in their unredeemed state is further related to the powers of evil in the expression "according to the ruler of the authority of the air." In typical Hebrew concept this would refer to Satan, who was often thought of as exercising his authority in the world and the upper regions short of the "heights," which would be heaven itself. This one who is described as the ruler of the authority of the air is identified as "the spirit which is now working in the sons of disobedience." He is an evil spirit, and he is constantly working in those who are marked by disobedience. The expression "the sons of disobedience" is a most graphic way of describing people. In the Greek language the term "son of" was so used. "Son of perdition" was a term which Paul used to describe one who is otherwise called "anti-christ." "Sons of disobedience" in this passage is the strongest possible term for describing those who are in rebellion against the rule and authority of God.

Verse 3, *in whom we also lived once in the lusts of our flesh, doing the things willed by the flesh and the fancy, and we were by nature children of wrath as the others also.* Paul does not exclude himself and his readers from the area of disobedience and sin. The pronoun "we" further identified by the adjective "all" seems to picture all believers. Some interpreters understand it to introduce Jewish believers in contrast to the Gentiles, understanding "you" in verse 2 to refer to Gentiles and "we" in verse 3 to refer to the Jews. This may be influenced by the fact that often in this epistle that is the case. Here, however, the expression "we, all of us" seems to be more comprehensive than just a reference to the Jews; it seems to embrace the Gentiles as well. At one time all were living in the midst of the sons of disobedience. They lived, giving expression to life in the realm of fleshly lusts.

The word translated "lusts" is a general word for desire. It was not basically a word of evil connotation, but when joined to the term "flesh" and when placed in this particular context it certainly conveys the idea of evil desires. The word "flesh" appears to be used with reference to the flesh with all its evil propensities, all its evil inclinations. Living, then, in the desires of sinful flesh, these people were doing constantly the things which the flesh wished. Whatever dictates the sinful flesh made they carried out. Joined to this is the word "fancies." It means considerations, that which comes to one's mind. Seeing the total again, Paul would say, "Once we too, all of us, lived in fleshly lusts, doing the wishes and the fancies of the flesh, and we were by nature children of wrath as the others also."

The term "children of wrath by nature" is the subject of much discussion. Just what did Paul mean by it? Some interpreters understand it to mean about what the psalmist meant when he spoke of being conceived in sin. This would look upon the noun "nature" as a modifier of the verb; hence "we were by nature children of wrath." Others understand the noun "nature" to be a qualifier of the word "children" which immediately precedes it. This would call for the expression to be rendered "we were children by nature of wrath." This would mean that in our natural state, unredeemed, we did those things which result in the wrath of God. We did them by natural inclination and apart from being instructed in such practice. This appears to be the more likely construction of the two. The significance would be that man apart from what Christ does for him in redemption gives expression by natural inclination to ways of life that result in the coming of God's wrath upon him. The word "wrath" is a word which pictures the fixed displeasure of God against all that is evil. It is a part of his righteous character as much as love is a part of his righteous character. In his righteousness he cannot tolerate sin. His displeasure is inevitably fixed against it. In the term "as the rest also" or "even as the rest" Paul joins himself and all his readers to those who had once engaged in a life of sin and disobedience. The displeasure of God is characteristically fixed against the evil that would infest our lives.

In verses 4–5 a strong adversative is introduced by the conjunction "but." *But God, being rich in mercy, because of his great love with which he loves us made us alive together with Christ even when we were dead in trespasses* (*by grace you are saved*). God enters into man's experience redemptively because he is rich in mercy. Even while he looks with displeasure upon man's sin he looks with mercy upon man himself. Because of this mercy and because of his love he rescues man from his state of spiritual death. The word "love" is the same one which was used in Ephesians 1:4. It speaks of the great value which God puts upon sinful man, and because of that value he moved redemptively into man's experience. There is in verse 5, chapter 2 a return to the idea of being dead expressed in verse 1. Even while we were dead in trespasses God loved us; he looked down upon us in mercy, and he made us alive together with Christ. Just as he raised Christ from the dead, so in connection with Christ he raises us from spiritual death. Attention has been given in Ephesians 1:13–14 to the concept of Paul that the believer is "in Christ." Here is a kindred idea, with a slightly different emphasis on what takes place in association "with

Christ." It is one of a series of such ideas running through the letters of Paul:

Crucified with Christ, Galations 2:20
Dead with Christ, Colossians 2:20
Buried with Christ, Romans 6:4
Made Alive with Christ, Ephesians 2:5
Raised with Christ, Colossians 3:1
Suffering with Christ, Romans 8:17
Glorified with Christ, Romans 8:17
Seated with Christ, Ephesians 2:6

The Greek preposition *sun* is joined with the verb in this expression "he made alive." It is a preposition of association. He made us alive with Christ. He has brought us then from the gloom of spiritual death into the light of spiritual life.

This is solely a work of grace on the part of God. That is observed in the expression "by grace you are saved." This is one of the most meaningful grammatical constructions in the New Testament. It is known as a perfect passive participle. The perfect tense in Greek is not the parallel of the perfect tense in English. In Greek the perfect tense speaks of a state of being. The entire tense describes action which has come to a state of being and exists in that finished state. Literally translated, the term would be "by grace you are in a state of having been saved." Apart from anything in the context to indicate otherwise, it is to be anticipated that a state of being is continuous in the absolute sense. This speaks with assurance of the security of that one who has been given spiritual life in association with Christ. He is in a state of having been saved so that he can never die spiritually again.

Verse 6, *and he raised* (*us*) *and seated* (*us*) *in the heav-*

enlies in Christ Jesus. God has made us alive. He has raised us up from our low estate of death and walking in trespasses and sins and has seated us in heavenly places in association with Christ Jesus. The state of the believer is a glorious state when compared to what he once was. All of this work of God in making alive, in raising up, in giving exalted position was for one specific purpose. That purpose is expressed in verse 7, *in order that he might demonstrate in coming ages the abounding riches of his grace in loving-kindness to us in Christ Jesus.* God's redemptive work was for the purpose of bringing about a means by which he could demonstrate the riches of his grace. The term translated "demonstrate" or "show" is a word which means to point out, to make clear. Throughout all ages to come God has a means of demonstrating the riches of his grace, and that means of demonstration is a redeemed people.

The term "grace" used here and elsewhere means, as it has been previously translated, "unmerited favor." It describes that which man has in Christ but which he could never merit or deserve on his own part. Because of his handicap, his limitation in his sin, man could never do that which would merit redemption. God, who by his righteous character is redemptive in nature, extends to man unmerited favor in rich quantity and quality which goes beyond any conception that man could have apart from divine revelation. All of this is in relationship to his loving-kindness or, perhaps a bit more exact, his graciousness, extended to us in relation to Christ.

Verses 8–9 pick up the expression of grace, repeating what was said in verse 5 and extending the idea, *for by grace you are in a state of having been saved through faith, and this not of yourself, of God the gift, not of works, lest any one should boast.* Grace is the favor which God bestows to bring redemption. Faith is man's means of appropriating that redemption. It is redemption that is "by grace through faith." The pronoun translated "this" (or sometimes translated "that") is a neuter pronoun. Both nouns "grace" and "faith" are feminine, so the pronoun can refer to neither of these nouns specifically. It refers to the *entire process* of redemption. Paul is not saying that grace is the gift of God or that faith is the gift of God. Rather, he is saying that the entire process—"redemption by grace through faith"—is God's gift. It does not have its source in men. It has its source in God. It is a plan of redemption which only a God of infinite wisdom and love could conceive and which only a God of infinite power could carry out. This redemption is a matter of grace and not of works, and that excludes boasting on the part of man. If man could attain to redemption by works, he would have something to boast about by way of his own accomplishment. That, however, is not the case. He is redeemed wholly as a matter of God's favor, and the only ground he has for boasting is the love of God, which would not leave man in sin without providing a way of redemption. This redemption which brings man from spiritual death to spiritual life is a blessing which defies human vocabulary to describe.

A Life of Good Works in Christ, 2:10

The life of the believer is a blessed experience in contrast to the life that was his before he came to experience redemption. One of the blessings of this redemption is a new life that is engaged in the all-consuming good works which God desires for his children. This idea appears in verse 10, *for we are his workmanship, having been created in Christ Jesus for good works, which God prepared beforehand in order that in them we might walk about.* We are his workmanship.

The Greek noun translated "workmanship" has been translated "poem." That is more a transliteration than translation. While the Greek word might mean a poem, it really was used for any finished product, whether a piece of literature, a painting, or a piece of marble sculpture. It is used in Romans 1:20 of God's "created things." The meaning here appears to be that we are God's finished product, having been created in relationship to Christ Jesus for good works. God has made us his finished product with the goal in mind that we should walk about in good works in contrast to the evil works which marked us in the unredeemed state. There is a rather tragic note in the statement "which God had prepared beforehand." While we were living in trespasses and sin, God had a complete area of good works in which we should have been walking about all of the time. One who has come to appreciate the fact that he is in Christ a new creation, having experienced God's redemptive re-creative work, could never be satisfied to go back to the old walk again.

II

The Propagation of Redemption

(2:11 to 3:21)

The most basic idea in the Christian religion is that of the provision of redemption for sinful men. Of almost equal importance as a basic note is the idea of the propagation of this plan of redemption. If there is one God and if this one God provides redemption for sinful men, it must follow that this redemption is available to all men. This is indeed a part of the "good news" (the gospel) itself. It is good news that God in Christ has provided a way of redemption for men apart from works, through grace, and in relationship to the life, death, resurrection, and heavenly priesthood of Jesus Christ. That is good news to needy men. If, however, this plan of redemption is not made known to men, all of it comes to naught. In this there is clearly seen the total evangelistic and missionary imperative of Christianity—the giving of the good news of this available redemption to all men everywhere.

Redemption for All Without Regard to Race, 2:11–13

Paul presents this idea of redemption for all men without regard to race by calling the attention of his Gentile readers to their status as Christians. They now enjoy the blessings of the fellowship of God which once they had not known at all. This glorious experience is outlined in terms of contrast between what once they were and what now they are.

Then (2:11–12), *Wherefore keep on remembering, that once you, the Gentiles in the flesh, who are called "Uncircumcision" by those who are called "Circumcision," in the flesh, made by hands, that you were at that time without Christ, alienated from the commonwealth of Israel, strangers to the covenants of the promise, having no hope and Godless in the world.* By the use of the word "wherefore" Paul links this discussion to the preceding paragraph, in which he has indicated that all who have come to know redemption have been re-created for a life of good works. Here he uses the present imperative to urge the Ephesian Christians never to forget what they were before they experienced that re-creative work of Christ. The translation "keep on remembering" is a very literal and very accurate rendering of the form. The word "once" in verse 11 will be echoed in verse 12 in the expression "at that time." It is a reference to the condition of the Gentiles before they came to experience redemption in Christ.

The entire expression in verse 11 is a most graphic picture of the contempt which the Jews held for the Gentiles. The contrast here is between the condition of the "Gentiles in the flesh" and the "Jews in the flesh." In Genesis 17:9–14 the record is given of God's making circumcision for every Jewish male eight days old and above a covenant mark between him and his people. Abraham, who was the object of the love and favor of God because of his faith, was commanded to accept circumcision for himself and for all his descendants after him in order that the covenant mark of God would be in their very flesh as a constant reminder. The esteem and honor which the Jews had for this ritual was a part of their very exclusiveness by which they shut themselves off from other people, and it was a part of the reason that they came to use as an expression of their contempt for the Gentiles the name "Uncircumcision." This, Paul indicates, was a name or epithet bestowed upon the Gentiles by the Jews, who were in turn called "Circumcision." But the covenant mark had lost its spiritual or religious significance and was only an artificial, superficial, man-made thing. Still the animosity and name calling existed between the two races.

In verse 12 Paul goes beyond the artificial and superficial distinction observed in verse 11 and describes the true spiritual condition of the Gentiles in their pre-Christian state. Several expressions are used to point up the tragedy of that condition. First, they were "without Christ." The expression translated "without" means apart from Christ. The total expression "you were at that time without Christ" will be observed most forcefully when set over against the contrasting expression in verse 13, "but now in Jesus Christ." So the term "without Christ" means the very opposite of Christian standing. Their condition was the very opposite of all that being in Christ means.

Second, they were "alienated from the commonwealth of Israel." By "alienated" Paul means that they were denied privileges which belonged to those who made up the commonwealth of Israel. The term "commonwealth" is one which speaks of a people who make up a body of citizenship. In the commonwealth of Israel God was looked upon as the ruler and the people were his subjects. Being the subjects of God, they were the recipients of certain privileges and blessings which God extended. These privileges and blessings, however, were not granted to those who were outside of the commonwealth.

Third, they were "strangers to the covenants of the promise." This is a bit stronger and a step beyond the last statement. It means that they were foreigners where the covenants of God were concerned. God had made his covenants. Ideally, they were covenants which related to the realm of the spiritual and which would ultimately be realized in relationship to the Redeemer that God would provide. In this sense they were promised covenants. They had served as a basis for courage and hope for the Jewish people, but the Gentiles were foreigners as far as these covenants were concerned. This alienation of the Gentiles from the commonwealth of Israel, this matter of being foreigners where the covenants were concerned, is a condition which speaks of Israel's failure. It was God's purpose to reveal himself to the world through the nation of Israel. Israel, however, became legalistic and exclusive. She took the approach, "We have the one true God; if you want him, you will have to become a Jew." The first part of their position was right. They had the one true God. The second part was wrong, and because of their error at that point they had erected barriers that kept the Gentiles away from the true religion and the true God known to the Jews.

Fourth, the Gentiles were "without hope" and "without God" in the world. These may be looked upon as separate descriptive terms, or they may be considered as two parts of one descriptive term. They were without hope in comparison to the Jews, who entertained hope for the future. Ideally, the Jewish religion looked forward in hope to the provision of redemption for their sins in a promised Messiah. In the day of Paul the Jews had come to a sad state as far as that hope was concerned, but even what little hope they had was more than that which the Gentiles had. Hope may relate to the life beyond as well. The idea of life beyond death, while dim in the Old Testament and Jewish thought, was a reality. For the Gentile there was little of such hope.

Indeed, some of the Greek philosophers held to the view of the immortality of the soul, but there was no idea of resurrection, and it was an idea which was far inferior to the element of hope which marked the Jews.

The expression "without God" is really an adjective. It is the plural form of the adjective which would describe people who had no God. The Gentile world had what it called gods. These gods were, in the conception of the Gentiles, little more than men, with all the evil inclinations, practices, and powers of men exaggerated to a very high degree. Even the purest systems of religion known to the Gentiles were so far removed from the religion of the true God that Paul could truthfully say that the Gentiles were "without God" altogether. The total picture is a very dark one; from all that can be known of the first century Gentile world it is a very accurate one.

Now (2:13), *But now in Christ Jesus you who once were far off have become near in the blood of Christ.* It would be difficult to find a word more packed with meaning and hope than this little word "now." It points to a condition which is the very opposite of all of that described in verse 12. Once they were foreigners to God's promised covenant, were denied the privileges that belonged to God's people, and could be described as those who were far off. Now the situation is altogether different. It is different because of what is involved in the term "in Christ Jesus." In verse 10 Paul had spoken of those who were "created in Christ Jesus." At many points in his previous discussion he has held up the idea of being in Christ.[1] Now the Gentiles who once were separated from Christ are in Christ. Those who were once aliens and for-

---

[1] In all his writings he uses the "in Christ" idea more than 160 times. In a few places it is difficult to tell whether "in him" refers to God or to Christ.

eigners are now a very part of the citizenship over which the true God is the ruler. This has become reality in relationship to the redemptive work of Christ.

The term "in the blood of Christ" is to be understood as a comprehensive reference to all that was involved in the experience of Jesus' incarnation, death, resurrection, and glorification. It is by means of this redemptive work which God has wrought in Christ and which he offers to sinful men on the basis of faith that the Gentiles have come to their present status. God provided complete and sufficient redemption in Christ. It had to follow that both Jews and Gentiles had equal access to that redemption.

Redemption Makes All Men One in Christ, 2:14–22

The different propositions presented and discussed by Paul in this epistle follow one after the other as natural corollaries. The *one* God has provided *one* way of redemption; it is for *all* men without regard to race; it must follow that it makes all men *one* in Christ. In him there is no east or west; in him there is no north or south. All who have come to redemption in him make up one great spiritual body in which every member is of equal standing and importance. This is true on the individual basis. It is true as well on the racial basis. Individually, one redeemed man has the same standing with God as every other redeemed man. Paul's major emphasis at this point, however, is on the basis of the racial idea, to the effect that in Christ Jew and Gentile have the same standing. Neither has a privileged position as against the other.

In Christ there is one new body. No longer are there two bodies—the Jews considered as having God, the Gentiles considered as not having God. Rather, there is one new body of God's people, and this new body is made up of believers, without regard to race, Jew or Gentile. Verse 14, *For he is our peace, who has made both to be one, and has broken down the middle wall of partition.* In Christ Jew and Gentile come to be at peace one with the other. In prophecy one of the names given to the Messiah was Prince of Peace (Isa. 9:6). When he was born, the heavenly hosts spoke of the fact that his coming meant "peace among men" (Luke 2:14). Paul affirms here that Christ *is* our peace. It is he who has made peace between two warring races, Jew and Gentile. He has made the two into one body by removing the barrier that stood between them. He has broken down the middle wall of partition or the dividing wall. This appears to have reference to the Temple in Jerusalem, in which a wall divided the court of the Gentiles from the court of the Jews. Into certain areas of the Temple the Gentiles could go in their observance of the Jewish religious life and in their searching for religious truths. There was, however, an area of the Temple which was forbidden to them, and on that stone wall was instruction warning Gentiles that they went beyond that wall on pain of death. Ideally, Paul says that Christ has broken down this dividing wall with the result that he has made of Jews who believe in him and Gentiles who believe in him one new people.

Verse 15 speaks more exactly of that which was illustrated by the middle wall of partition, *having abolished in his flesh the enmity, that is the law of commandments in ordinances, in order that he might create in himself of the two one new man, making peace.* The great barrier which had stood between the Jews and the Gentiles was that which Paul calls "the law of commandments in ordinances." It was the legalistic system including ceremonial laws and health laws which had set the Jews apart as a separate nation and which had kept them separated from the Gentiles. A part of the initiative in this separation was found in both groups. The Jews were proud of their laws and their institutions, and this produced the spirit of exclusiveness which shut out the Gentiles and ultimately caused the Jew to look upon the Gentile with contempt. On the other hand, there was much about the Jewish ceremonial, particularly related to health and food laws and practices, which repelled the Gentile. Even the rite of circumcision was repulsive to the Gentile, because he honored the physical body and he looked upon that practice as mutilation.

All of this together created a barrier that stood between the two races. Paul's view is that "in his flesh," that is, in his incarnation and redemptive work, Christ has abolished that barrier by setting aside and making meaningless as far as religious matters are concerned all of these practices which had been precious to the Jews but repulsive to the Gentiles. Some of the practices were indeed continued by Jews who became Christians, but from Paul's viewpoint they were continued only as health measures or as traditional measures and not because of their religious significance. From the viewpoint of religious significance they were set aside through the redemptive work of Christ, and when they were set aside, peace was made between the Jews who believed in Christ and the Gentiles who believed in Christ.

This same idea is continued in verse 16, *and might reconcile them both in one body to God through the cross, having slain the enmity by it.* Through the redemptive work of the cross Christ has put to death that which constituted enmity between Jew and Gentile. He has reconciled them one to another, and he has brought them as one spiritual body into right relationship to God. A twofold reconciliation is effected. They are reconciled one to the other by means of the cross of Christ, and in turn they both, Jew and Gentile, come to be reconciled to God through the cross. Even with all of his history rich in religious experience, the Jew had come to be about as far from God as was the Gentile. He had come to the place that all of his religious devotion was merely a matter of form which had no inner spiritual content. He needed to be reconciled to God. The Gentile steeped in the evil of his sin and his pagan practices needed to be reconciled to God. There was in both that which made a righteous God look upon them with displeasure. By means of the cross Christ has brought them into such state that God can look upon them with favor. They are reconciled to him, and they are reconciled one to the other.

Verse 17 emphasizes the work of Christ in this redemption in the statement, *He came and preached peace to you who were far off* (*the Gentiles*), *and peace to those that were near* (*the Jews*). He preached peace in the days of his earthly ministry, but his most effective sermon on peace was the cross itself. It was by means of the cross that he made peace between those who once had been bitter enemies but now have come to know Christ and his love and to experience love one for the other.

Verse 18, *For through him we both have our introduction in one Spirit unto the Father*. This concludes Paul's emphasis on the fact that Jew and Gentile are made one new body in Christ. This appears to be a reference to the redemptive work of the Trinity. As such it echoes the extended discussion of chapter 1. Through Christ both Jew and Gentile have their introduction in one Spirit to the Father. Lenski [2] does not see this as a reference to the Trinity. He understands Paul to be saying that God in Christ has made Jew and Gen-

---

[2] R. C. H. Lenski, *The Interpretation of St. Paul's Epistles to the Galatians, to the Ephesians, and to the Philippians* (Columbus: Wartburg Press, 1937), p. 448.

tile to be one body and that they are characterized by one spirit, that is, one mind and heart in relationship to Christ. Other interpreters, however, understand the word "spirit" to be a reference to the Holy Spirit. We have our introduction to the Father in the realm of the one Holy Spirit and through the redemptive work of Christ.

This new body is built on one foundation. In verses 19–22 Paul conceives of this new body of Christ's people as a building, and all of it, the Jewish part and the Gentile part, is built upon one foundation. The body is one as to its nature, one as to its Redeemer, one as to its foundation.

Verse 19, *So then you are no longer strangers and foreigners, but you are fellow citizens with the saints, and household members of God.* Paul was proud of his Roman citizenship. Here he conceives of a higher citizenship—a citizenship which has the eternal God as the ruler and all of his people as subjects. By the work of Christ the Gentiles are no longer strangers to that citizenship and alienated from it. They have come to be fellow citizens with the others who were God's people. They have come to be members of the very household of God.

Verse 20, *being built upon the foundation of the apostles and prophets, Christ Jesus himself being chief cornerstone.* There is an element of transition from the idea of a body of people to the idea of a building. This building made up of Gentiles and Jews has as its foundation the apostles, the prophets, and Christ himself. It appears to be futile to try to determine whether or not the word "prophet" refers to the prophets of the ancient Jewish religious system. If that is the case, Paul would be joining together the old Jewish religious system (represented by the prophets) and the new Jewish religious system (represented by the apostles) and relating both to Christ as the most important part of the foundation. While that is possible, it seems a bit unlikely. If Paul had that in mind, a reversal of the terms would have been more natural, that is, prophets and apostles. It seems more likely that both apostles and prophets refer to the ones who were the first proclaimers of the work of God based on Christ. The apostles were those "sent with a message" concerning God's redemptive work in Christ. They had seen the Lord, and many of them, at least, worked miracles. The prophets were those who were the "spokesmen," that is, the preachers of God. They spoke, giving evidence that their speaking was under the direct influence of the Holy Spirit.

Upon these workers this new building of God is founded, with Christ Jesus himself being the most important part of the foundation. This is not to be thought of in terms of conflict with Paul's statement in 1 Corinthians 3:11 that there can be no other foundation than Jesus Christ. The setting of the Corinthian letter was altogether different. Paul was contrasting his work with that of Apollos or any other worker and was indicating that in the matter of building human agents are quite secondary in importance. The thing which is of greatest importance is the foundation on which they build, and that is Jesus Christ himself. In this Ephesian passage the pre-eminent position of Christ is observed in the use of the word translated "chief cornerstone."

The use of the cornerstone is a matter of much difference of opinion. One interpreter views this as the chief stone which would hold together the supporting arch in some building. Another interpreter would think of it as the very basic foundation stone on which other stones would be placed, still as a part of the general foundation. Still other interpreters think of this stone as the one which indicates the type of architecture which is to be used throughout the entire building. Whichever view is right, the pre-eminent place in the foundation on which this new house is built belongs to Christ. It it interesting to observe Paul's change in the figure. In the first part he sees Christ as one who through his cross *builds* the separate materials (Jew and Gentile) into a house. In this part he changes his figure and sees Christ as the *foundation* upon which the house is built. It is not an exaggerated idea that Christ is both builder and foundation.

Verse 21, *in relationship to whom each building, fitly joined together, increases into a holy dwelling place in the Lord.* One can hardly be dogmatic about the meaning of the term "each building." Some understand it to mean each individual church or each individual Christian community. Each individual church fitly joined together in all its constituent members comes to be the dwelling place of God. Others understand the term "each building" to speak of the Jews as one building and the Gentiles as another building. These two buildings come to be properly joined together or fitly joined together, and this results in a dwelling place for God. Grammatically, the former translation is more attractive, but in this total context and carrying out the illustration that Paul has used the latter interpretation is more attractive. By this we would understand Paul to say that God no longer has a Jewish house in which he dwells. He has a new house made up of Jews and Gentiles and built on Christ as the foundation, and that is his dwelling place.

What Paul has said of the entire building, both Jew and Gentile, in verses 20–21 he says particularly of the Gentile's part in verse 22, *in whom you also are being built together into a dwelling place of God in the Spirit.* It is fitting that having started his discussion in verse 11 with an emphasis upon the Gentiles he should close his discussion with an emphasis upon the Gentiles. Because of this contrast which has been observed all through the discussion one is tempted to translate the Greek word *kai* "even" rather than "also," that is, "in whom even you are being built together for a dwelling place of God." Even the once despised Gentiles are recognized now as a growing house, as a dwelling place for God. If, however, the word *kai* must be rendered "also," the force of contrast is not lost, and what Paul said of the entire spiritual body in verse 21 he says of the Gentile part of the body in verse 22. In the making known of redemption to men it must be made clear that it is for all without regard to race, and it makes all believers one body in Christ.

Twentieth-century Christians do well to look to the existing situation today and remember that this redemption is still for all men and that the original evangelistic and missionary imperative is still in force. To far too great an extent Christianity has slipped today into an error which is the opposite of that of the Jews. The error of the Jews was in thinking that God's redemptive mercy was for Jews only—the Gentiles were "off limits." Far too many Christians today (in practice if not in theory) look upon the Jews as being "off limits," and no effort is made to face them with their responsibility to God's fulfilment of his offer to provide a Redeemer. In many instances when a religious census has been made in preparation for a special evangelistic effort, the names of Jews have been put aside as being outside the list of prospects. This is not the New Testament approach. According to the New Testament, the only redemptive hope for the Jew is Jesus Christ, and every man without Christ is the object of Christian witnessing. We default in our responsibility if we fail to make positive efforts to win the Jews to Christ just as we try to win the Gentiles—one by one. In Romans 9–11 Paul saw the glory of God's plan in the fact that the gospel was brought to the Gentiles by way of the Jews. He envisioned the day when in turn the gospel would be brought to the Jews by means of the Gentiles. Until we do that we are failing in a part of our mission.

Redemption Revealed to Men Through Men, 3:1–13

It is an axiom of Christian history that "God's plan is a man." God has chosen to carry out his work among men through the agency of men. That was true in his dealings with men by way of revelation and instruction in the religious history of Israel. It was true in his work in the days of Christ, when he chose men to be with him that he might instruct them and send them out to do his work. When he was leaving the world at the time of his ascension, Christ gave to men the commission for the proclamation of redemption. When the time came that the gospel could be made known effectively to the Gentile world, his plan was to use men for that purpose. It was not only necessary that the one God include the Gentiles in his one way of redemption. It was also necessary for him to establish a means of revealing that redemption to them. In Ephesians 3:1–13 Paul discusses this fact and the related fact that he himself was the instrument chosen of God to make known that revelation to the Gentile world. We are already acquainted with this idea from our knowledge of Paul's activities as recorded in the book of Acts, from our knowledge of the decision of the church council as recorded in Acts 15, and from Paul's frequent references in his epistles to his ministry to the Gentiles.

Verse 1, *For this cause I, Paul, the prisoner of Christ in behalf of you the Gentiles.* This apparently does not mean that Paul was the prisoner of Christ in the sense in which he often spoke of himself as being a "slave" of Christ. It appears to mean literally that he was in jail, that is, under arrest. This is further indicated in Ephesians 6:20, when Paul speaks of himself as an "ambassador in chains." He has come to that situation because of his ministry to the Gentiles. A review of his activities as recorded in Acts 21:15 to 28:31 is helpful at this point. While he was in Jerusalem he was seen in the company of a Gentile from Ephesus (Acts 21:29). The Jewish people accused him of taking the Gentile into the Temple. This led to his arrest by the Jews, his rescue from the Jews by the Romans, the long period of imprisonment at Caesarea, and ultimately the voyage to Rome to stand trial before Caesar himself. Paul was, then, very literally a prisoner in the interest of the Gentiles. At the end of verse 1 there is a definite break in the flow of the discussion. Paul starts out to speak of some activity on his own part related to the previously discussed idea of redemption for the Gentiles. He breaks the discussion at the end of verse 1 and apparently comes back to state his original thought in verses 14–19. From verses 2 through 13 Paul turns aside to speak of the fact of his appointment as a messenger of redemption to the Gentiles. The missionary imperative which he felt for the Gentiles is an integral part of the missionary imperative of the Christian religion in its total expression. God's way is that this plan of redemption shall be made known to men through men.

Verse 2, *if indeed you have heard of the stewardship of the grace of God which has been given to me with reference to you.* This indicates that there were many of the readers of this epistle who might not be acquainted with this special trusteeship of God's grace that Paul should be the minister to the Gentiles. The Ephesian Christians certainly would be acquainted with that, since Paul had preached there for three years. If, however, this is a circular letter to be used in other churches in Asia Minor, there would likely be many who were not acquainted with that particular responsibility of Paul as it was reinforced by the decision of the church leaders in the conference at Jerusalem (Acts 15:22–29; Gal. 2:9). Paul feels that it is necessary for him to give some extended explanation of his mission to the Gentiles.

Verses 3–5, *that according to revelation the mystery was made known to me, just as I wrote previously briefly, facing which you will be able to understand my understanding in the mystery of Christ, which in other generations was not made known to the sons of men, as now it has been revealed to his holy apostles and prophets in the Spirit.* The expression "as I wrote previously briefly" may be a reference to Paul's statement in Ephesians 1:9 relative to the making known of the "mystery" of God's will. Either that is the case or he is referring to some previously written letter which the recipients of this letter will already have read. As indicated in earlier discussion, the term "mystery" refers to something which could not be known apart from divine revelation. Paul speaks of the revelation which made known to him this mystery as it is related to Christ, a mystery which had not been revealed in other generations but now has been revealed to Christ's apostles and prophets. It is in the realm of the activity of the Holy Spirit that this revelation has been made.

Verse 6, *that the Gentiles are fellow heirs and fellow body members and fellow partakers of the promise in Christ Jesus through the gospel.* This is the one great mystery which distinguishes the religion of Christ—its universal scope. The good news of redemption in Christ was not to be limited to the Jews. It was to be made known to the Gentiles, with the result that they would be, along with the Jews, fellow heirs, fellow body members, and fellow sharers in the promise of Christ. Jesus himself in the days of his earthly ministry had indicated as much, but people were not willing to receive it. That is evident by the experience of Jesus upon his return to Nazareth following his baptism and the response of the people to his teaching in the synagogue (Luke 4:16–30). When an opportunity was given to him to speak in the synagogue, he turned in the Scriptures to Isaiah 61:1–3. He read the passage which spoke of God's Spirit coming upon his Messiah and anointing him to preach the good news. When he had finished reading the passage, Jesus opened his sermon by the bold declaration that the people of Nazareth were seeing a fulfilment of that Scripture in himself. He was the one who was anointed by God himself to preach the good news.

He continued by showing that this mercy of God was not to be limited to the Jews; it was to be for the Gentiles as well. From Old Testament history he illustrated his idea that God's mercy was for the Gentiles. He said that there were many Jewish widows in the days of Elijah, but when God wanted to show special mercy to a widow he selected a Gentile widow in Zarephath of Sidon as a means of demonstrating his mercy. Likewise, Jesus said there were many Jewish lepers in the day of Elisha, but when God wanted to show special mercy to a leper he extended that mercy to a Gentile, Naaman of Syria. The people were so furious that Jesus would say God cared in any such special way for the Gentiles that they would not let him finish his sermon. They rushed him out of the synagogue and attempted to put him to death by pushing him over the precipice. Paul, too, insisted that God's mercy was for the Gentiles and that it was an essential part of that which had been revealed to him that the Gentiles are to be an integral part of the people of God.

In verse 7 Paul speaks particularly of his having been made a minister according to the principle of God's grace and in line with the working of God's power. He was made a minister of that very gospel or good news of redemption for all men in Christ. In verse 8 he conceives of himself as the very least of all the saints; yet this gracious gift of God was made to him that he should be privileged to preach to the Gentiles the untraceable riches of Christ. It is no mock humility when Paul speaks of himself as "less than the least" or "the very least of all saints." He felt his unworthiness because of what his life had been as one who persecuted the Christians and tried to destroy the work of Christ; yet in the wisdom of God he was the instrument chosen of God to be the great preacher and missionary of the first Christian century. Paul never ceased to give expression to his own amazement that he had been chosen of God for this service.

One of the most suggestive terms used by Paul with reference to the gospel is the expression in verse 8, "the untraceable riches of Christ." This was a word used by the Greek people to describe a road or a trail which could be traced a part of the way that it had come but not all the way. The beginnings of the trail would be lost, and it could not be traced back to its origin. Paul speaks of the riches of Christ as a trail or a road which is lost in the infinite depths of the divine plan and love of God. It can be traced a part of the way back toward its beginning, but finite man loses the trail. In imagination one traces the "trail" a part of the way. It can be traced by the Mount of Olives from which Jesus ascended to heaven. From there it goes by an empty tomb in the garden of Joseph of Arimathea. From there it goes by a skull-shaped hill and three crosses as a marker. Beyond that it passes a garden named Gethsemane, which speaks of the agony of Jesus. Farther on it can be traced by a stable-manger in Bethlehem where the Redeemer was born.

On back beyond that traces can be found in the meaningful sacrificial system of the Temple in Jerusalem and beyond that the tabernacle in the wilderness. Pushing farther back and growing dim, though still traceable, it can be marked by the meaningful sacrifices of Abraham and on to the very beginning of man's recorded history in the Garden of Eden. It can be traced by the sacrifices that were made that the shame of man might be covered and by the promise of God that one day he would provide a covering for man's total sin and shame. On back beyond the Garden of Eden in the purpose of God before the world was created one can find evidence of this "trail." But there and beyond there it eludes man's ability to follow and becomes "the untraceable riches of Christ." Such was the gospel of redemption that God would make known to all men, and Paul was his chosen instrument to make it known to the Gentiles.

Verse 9 continues this responsibility of Paul as the revealer of the way of redemption. It was God's purpose that he should *make all men see what is the stewardship of the mystery which for ages has been hidden in God who created all things*. There appears to be little that is new in this verse. Redemption is for all men. It is looked upon as a trusteeship. It has been hidden in past ages in the wisdom of God, but now it is made clear through the divine revelation.

Further expression of God's purpose in this is seen in verse 10, *in order that now to rulers and authorities in the heavenlies the manifold wisdom of God might be made known through the church*. Apparently the reference here to rulers and authorities in heavenly places has to do with the angelic order. In the New Testament angels are spoken of as having an interest in the redemptive work of God in Christ (1 Peter 1:12). Here Paul appears to say that they come to an understanding of the many-sided wisdom of God as the church performs its purpose of proclaiming the good news of redemption. There appears to be in Paul's mind a sense in which the wisdom of God cannot be understood even by the angels apart from the fulfilment of the evangelistic and missionary purpose which he has for his church. As his people make known his way of redemption and as others receive that way of redemption, even the angels come to a greater knowledge of and appreciation for the great wisdom of God.

Verse 11, *according to the eternal purpose which he made in Christ Jesus our Lord.* The expression would literally be rendered "according to a purpose of the ages." The word which is translated "eternal" has various uses in the New Testament. Sometimes it refers to that which has a beginning in time and never ends. Sometimes it refers to that which has existed without reference to a time when it started. At other times it refers to that which existed before time as man knows it started. That appears to be the significance of this usage. It speaks of God's purpose which existed even before the creation of the world and of man. It is more than simply ageless purpose. It is more closely related to the idea involved in the phrase "before the foundation of the world" (Eph. 1:4). This eternal purpose God made in Jesus Christ our Lord. The making known of the wisdom of God to angelic servants and through the church is all in line with God's eternal purpose which has revealed in Paul's time this mystery of redemptive mercy to the Gentiles.

Verse 12, *in whom we have boldness and access in confidence through faith in him.* Here, as in other instances, the Greek text has a definite article indicating "the faith." It may be merely the use of the definite article with the noun, having no particular emphasis, but most likely it is another instance in which the article has the force of the possessive pronoun, that is, "our faith." The pronoun translated "him" is in the genitive case. Apparently it is the objective genitive, justifying the translation "through our faith in him." It is faith which is placed in Jesus Christ that gives to the believer the sense of confidence in his approach to God. The word translated "boldness" means literally "freedom to speak." In Christ we come to God in perfect freedom and with no spirit of reluctance or fear that we will not be received. The word translated "access" may also be translated "introduction." The Greek term expresses the idea of one's being led into the presence of another. It was used in Paul's day of one who was introduced into the presence of royalty, that is, one who was presented at the court of the king. In Christ we have our "presentation to royalty," that is, our introduction to the Father. And it is an experience in which we stand not in trembling and fear, but in confidence of favorable reception. The favorable reception is due not to our worthiness to be presented, but to the worthiness of the One who presents us. He has provided redemption, forgiveness, covering for our sins. It is with a consciousness of such provision that we stand in the presence of God.

Verse 13, *Wherefore, I ask not to faint in my tribulations on behalf of you which (tribulation) is your glory.* The exact meaning of Paul is not made clear in this verse. The translation is a literal translation of the text. Two possibilities are present. One is that Paul is making request that he will not faint in the midst of his tribulation. If this is the meaning, apparently the verb "I ask" indicates prayer, and the middle voice of the verb indicates the idea, "I ask for myself that I not faint." This is entirely possible. There is, however, a second possibility, and that is that Paul is making intense prayer to God that the readers of the letter will not faint when they hear of his tribulation. If this is the meaning, the translation would more properly be, "Wherefore I ask (God) that you not faint at my tribulations." Still a third idea is that Paul means, "I ask you not to faint."

Knowing Paul's spirit of endurance in the midst of difficulties, one is inclined to think that the second interpretation is likely the correct one. Paul is not fearful of his own ability to face up to his tribulations. He is concerned lest his readers become too discouraged when they hear that the great preacher and missionary is a prisoner and has been in prison for several years. It would be easy for people of spiritual immaturity to misinterpret such a situation and to take the position, "If he were really doing the work of God, would God permit him to experience imprisonment?" Paul's concern is that they shall have another understanding of his tribulation, and that is that his tribulation is really in their interest and to their glory. It is in their interest in the sense that he is a prisoner because of his ministry to the Gentiles. This has been discussed previously. Again, his tribulations are to their glory in the sense that through his ministry to the Gentiles, difficult as it is, they have come to know the redemptive work of God in Christ.

The word translated "tribulations" is one of the most meaningful Greek terms when used in Christian application. It is a word which referred to external pressures which would appear to crush and to ruin. From the Christian concept such external pressures do not crush and ruin. They serve to press one into a form which will make him of more effective service. The word was used of pressing grapes. Into a large stone vat the grapes were placed. On top of the grapes was placed a large, flat stone. Men or work animals walked around on top of this stone, crushing the grapes to a pulp. Sometimes they dispensed with the large, flat stone and trampled the grapes directly with their feet! This was known as "treading the wine press." As the grapes were crushed, the juice ran out of holes at the bottom of the wine press and was caught in containers placed there. A person not acquainted with the process and the purpose of such activity might gain the impression that the grapes were being ruined. Such was not the case; they were being pressed into a different form for more effective service.

In like manner, this same word was used for the grain mill. A large, round, flat stone was placed on the ground. On top of it was placed a second large, round stone like a wheel with a hole in the center. Grain was poured into this hole. The round, flat stone on top was then turned around and around by human power or animal power, and as it turned, the grain was drawn in between the two stones and ground into flour. It dropped out around the edges into containers or upon cloth placed there to catch it. Here again the uninitiated might think the wheat was being ruined. Such was not the case; it was being transformed for more effective use. So the Christian concept of tribulation, pressure, difficulty is that such does not ruin. It only puts one into a different form for more effective service to God. If the readers of the Ephesian letter will accept Paul's imprisonment from that viewpoint, they will not be disturbed to the point of fainting when they hear of his long imprisonment.

Redemption's Ultimate Goal, 3:14–21

This redemption which the one God has made possible and available to all men through Christ and mediated from one man to another has an ultimate goal of glorious design. Apparently it was this goal which Paul started to name in verse 1 when he said, "For this cause I, Paul . . ." It was at the mention of his being a prisoner in the interest of the Gentiles that he felt constrained to turn aside and explain that mission and ministry before going on to give expression to the ultimate goal of this redemption which makes all men one body or house built upon Christ as the foundation. He takes up this idea in verses 14–15, *For this cause I bow my knees unto the Father, from whom every fatherhood* (*or family*) *in heaven or on earth is named.* Paul bows his knees in prayer. The content of his prayer will be given in verses 16–19. The One to whom his prayer is directed is the Heavenly Father. The idea of God as Father has a particular significance in New Testament usage. It is true that in Old Testament usage God was sometimes spoken of as Father, but the emphasis was more on the idea of God as the Father of the group or the nation. In the New Testament the distinct idea is on God as the Father of the individual. This is the supreme Father of all men. He is the source of everything that speaks of fatherhood or family relationship, whether in heaven or upon the earth. Apart from the idea of God as Father and his subjects as children, one could hardly have the idea of fatherhood and family life on the earthly level. There is, of course, the clan idea or the father-mother-child relationship out in the pagan world where the true God is not known. It is Paul's idea, however, that even that concept is possible only because of the fact that the eternal God is a great Father and his subjects are his children.

Verses 16–19 express the prayer that Paul makes to God on behalf of his readers. There are several petitions in the prayer, but all of them point to the ultimate goal of redemption, which is the capacity of the redeemed to appropriate the full spiritual blessings which are in Christ and are meaningful in the light of the fourfold measurement of the love of Christ: breadth, length, height, and depth. Verse 16 introduces the content of the prayer, *that he might give to you according to the wealth of his glory to be strengthened by power through his Spirit with reference to the inner man.* Paul's prayer is that the Ephesian Christians may be divinely strengthened in their inner spiritual life in proportion to the riches (or the wealth) of the glory of God. He is a God who is able to give abundantly all that which is needed by his people. He has power to give strength in place of their weakness, and it is Paul's desire that through the working of the Holy Spirit in the inner spiritual life of the believers they may come to experience this power.

Verse 17 continues the petition, *in order that Christ may dwell through faith in your hearts.* This petition is parallel to the former petition rather than being related to it as a modifier. It is not Paul's idea that they shall be strengthened with reference to the inner man in order that Christ may dwell in their hearts through faith. It is rather that he expresses parallel ideas in a prayer that God will give to the readers the two things expressed: strength by power through the Spirit's working and realization of the indwelling presence of Christ. Christ dwells in the hearts of men through faith, and here again in direct manner, and yet without making a particular point of it, Paul presents the three persons of the Trinity. The Father grants to the believers the ability to be strengthened through the working of the Holy Spirit in them and to realize through faith the indwelling presence of Christ. The next expression in the text may be a part of this clause, or it may go forward to the following one. It appears naturally to go forward to the next expression, and hence it is so translated.

Verses 18–19, *in order that being rooted and grounded in love, you may have sufficiency to comprehend with all the saints what is the breadth and length and heighth and depth, moreover to know the love of Christ surpassing knowledge, in order that you may be filled with reference to all the fulness of God.* This continues the petition which Paul introduced in verse 14 with the statement, "I bow my knees to the Father." It may be directly related to that verb in the sense that "I bow my knees to the Father in order that you may have sufficiency to understand," etc. It may, however, be a modifier of the purpose clause which has just preceded it. If this is true, Paul says that he bows his knees to the Father that the readers may be strengthened through the work of the Holy Spirit and may realize the indwelling presence of Christ in order that they may have power to understand the love of Christ. Either construction can be readily understood as a part of Paul's habit of writing. He uses both structures in other places. However one looks on the particular syntax, the real force of the construction is ultimately the same. The ultimate force is that being rooted and grounded in love the reader may be strengthened to understand (or have sufficiency to understand) the love of Christ in its fourfold measurement.

There is the possibility of a double metaphor in Paul's expression "rooted and grounded." The former may reflect the idea of a tree that has its roots deep in the earth with the resulting stability. The second word was used for foundations of buildings. It pictures a building that has a firm foundation and cannot be shaken. In both instances love is the ground or soil in which the tree is rooted and upon which the house is built. This is love in the comprehensive sense—love for God which cannot stop there but reaches out to include one's fellow man as well. Rooted like a tree in the soil of love, founded like a building upon the firm ground of love, they will have power or sufficiency to understand this love of Christ. This sufficiency they will have in association with all the saints. From the beginning of the revelation of God's love in Christ, his people have come one after the other to a genuine understanding or appreciation for the meaningful love of Christ. This is an experience which they have in common, and Paul's prayer for the readers of the Ephesian letter is that they, too, shall come to share this appreciation.

The word translated "understand" or "comprehend" means literally "to receive down." It appears to have the force of the idea "to grasp." It is Paul's desire that the Ephesian readers have the ability to grasp the significance of the love of Christ in its breadth, length, height, and depth. We are not to explore each of these suggested measurements with a view to detailed interpretation. Apparently this is another instance of Paul's piling up words for the sake of dramatic expression. How could the love of Christ be described more comprehensively than by reference to its breadth, length, height, and depth? It is a tribute to the all-encompassing love of Christ, and one's imagination is left to its own inclination in exploring the ideas suggested. How high does the love of Christ reach? How deep does the love of Christ go? How far out does the love of Christ go? To what length does the love of Christ go?

This exalted expression concerning the love of Christ is indicated further in Paul's statement in verse 19, "to know the surpassing-knowledge love of Christ." His desire (and his prayer for the Ephesian readers) is that they may have sufficiency to grasp the fourfold measurement of the love of Christ and to know from the viewpoint of personal experience this love, which in reality surpasses knowledge. The love of Christ may be known and experienced by man, but there is a sense in which the love of Christ goes beyond man's finite knowledge. It is beyond the power of finite mind to know all that is involved in the redemptive love of Christ. Such was the case with Nicodemus (John 3:1–15). Nicodemus confessed that he did not understand how a mature man could experience birth a second time, even in the spiritual sense of birth. Jesus illustrated by the wind. He called Nicodemus' attention to the fact that Nicodemus could not know the source from which the wind came or the ultimate destination to which it went, but he could experience the present reality of it. In the same way, he said, one may not understand all the initial processes in the redemptive love of God and he may not understand all the ultimate reach of that redemptive love, but he can experience the present reality of it. So here Paul feels that the believer may know experientially the love of Christ, boundless in nature, even while he cannot know all that is involved in it.

The end result of all of this petition that they shall be strengthened by the Spirit, conscious of the indwelling Christ, and strong to grasp the meaning of the love of Christ is that they shall be filled with reference to all the fulness of God. This gives expression to a concept of Paul which seems to elude man's ability to understand. It may be oversimplification, and yet it can hardly be expressed otherwise, to say that the idea is that they shall come to experience fully all of God's purpose for them in bringing them to redemption from sin and to sonship to God. In this they will be filled with all the fulness of God.

This lengthy and lofty discussion of the theme of God's plan of redemption and its propagation to men closes with a doxology (vv. 20–21) just as it opened with a doxology (1:3–14). Here, as in chapter 1 and as it will appear in other places (5:14–21), Paul bursts into song. Verses 20–21, *Now to the one who is able above all things to do abundantly more than we ask or think, according to the power which is now working in him, to him the glory in the church and in Christ Jesus unto all the generations forever and ever. Amen.* This doxology expresses a tribute of glory to God in the realm of the church and in the realm of Christ Jesus forever and ever. God is the one who is able to do abundantly more than we ask or think. The expression "above all things" makes it all the more comprehensive. In the unlimited sense when absolutely everything is considered, God is still able to do abundantly more than we ask or think.

The word translated "abundantly more" is a word made up of four separate particles meaning "above, out of, and around." God is able to do "above, out of, and around" all things which we ask or think. When faith is inclined to falter in thinking that it may be asking too much of God, Paul would remind us that God is able to do abundantly more than all things which we ask him to do. To make the case even stronger, Paul says that God is able to do abundantly more than all the things which we might *think* to ask him to do. Faith is not to falter at the point of refusing to ask God, even when the thought is present. Faith is to recognize that God has the power to do far more than anything we may ask him to do or may even consider asking him to do.

He is able to do this "according to the power which is now working in him." This is apparently the power which he set into operation in the redemptive work of Christ. Attention was given to it particularly in Ephesians 1:19–20. It is the same kind of power which brought about the resurrection of Christ from the dead. That power of God is an inward-working energy in the believer. Attention has been called many times to the fact that the Greek word translated "power," if transliterated into English, would be our word "dynamite." We are not to weaken the term by so rendering it. We are merely to see our English word as an illustration of the idea of tremendous power. The word translated "working," if transliterated into English, would be "energizing within." So God is able to do more than we ask or think to ask, and he is able to do it according to the power which is now working energetically within us, that is, within the heart and life of every believer.

To such a God of redemptive, transforming, energizing

power, praise is attributed in the total realm of the church (his redeemed people) and in the total realm of his Son Christ Jesus, who has made all of this redemptive experience possible for the church. This is unending praise. Paul multiplies words and expressions to make that clear. It is praise to God unto all the generations "of the age of the ages." This is an idiom in Greek which would be rendered literally in English "unto all the generations forever and ever." Properly the doxology closes with the word "Amen." In English this is a transliteration of the Greek word which in turn was a transliteration of a Hebrew word related to the verb for being. It is understood in English by the optative form of the verb "to be," that is, "So let it be." As such it expresses the emotion of the reverent heart as he looks to the redemptive God and his work in Christ.

III

The Application of Redemption in Church Life

(4:1–16)

Here begins the second major division of the epistle to the Ephesians. As previously indicated, this section is practical in nature, and in it Paul sets out the ethical implications of the doctrinal truth discussed in chapters 1–3. It is to be remembered that the division is one that is organizational only. In the mind of Paul doctrine and ethics go hand in hand. One is not to be separated from the other in such way as to leave the impression that one would be sufficient without the other. Through three chapters he has discussed the theme of redemption in Christ for all men. Now through three chapters he will show what this truth means when it is applied in the everyday life of man, whether in personal life or in group relationship.

The starting point is not with its application in personal life but rather with its application in group relationship. Here Paul takes up again the theme of the body which is made up of all believers. He shows something of the nature of this body and something of God's purpose for it. Christ is the head of this body. All who are his fill out the remaining members of the body, and everything which they do is for the one purpose of building up the entire body. This is a beautiful concept. It is a favorite illustration on the part of Paul, one that he used in larger measure in 1 Corinthians 12–14.

The Unity Which the Spirit Produces, 4:1–6

Verse 1, *Therefore I exhort you, I the prisoner in the Lord, to walk worthily of the calling of which you have been called.* The word "therefore" is a resumptive particle. It is not likely to be understood in immediate relationship to the reference to the church in 3:21. It may be a reference to all that God has done for the Gentiles through the processes of grace and hence related to 3:6–19. Most likely, however, it is a particle which forms the bridge between chapters 1–3 and chapters 4–6. It relates all that Paul has said in the doctrinal section to all that he will say in this practical section. The verb "I exhort" was often used by the Greek people with a sense of admonition, "I admonish." More often it was used in the sense that it is here translated, "I exhort"; and quite often in the New Testament it comes to have a force of entreating and may be rendered "I entreat."

The object of the verb is the personal pronoun "you," which has reference to all the readers of this epistle. They are, for the most part, Gentile readers who have come to be a part of the people of God through the redemptive grace which God has extended to them. Again Paul reminds them, as he did in 3:13, that he suffers imprisonment because of his ministry in their interest. He is a prisoner in the Lord because of the ministry which he has extended in bringing the gospel to the Gentiles, but he considers it an exalted privilege. The use of the locative expression "in the Lord" rather than "of the Lord" suggests this idea. Paul does not make the statement as an appeal to their sympathy. Rather, he makes it to encourage them to be loyal to the Lord along the lines which he is going to suggest to them. His loyalty to the Lord has resulted in imprisonment; they are to be encouraged by his example and are to be loyal to the Lord whatever it may cost them.

This loyalty which he has in mind for them is introduced by the expression "to walk worthily of the calling of which you have been called." This is the same term "to walk about" which Paul used in chapter 2. Once they walked about in trespasses and sin while it was the purpose of God that they should walk about in good works. Now he encourages them to walk about in a manner worthy of the calling which they have experienced. This, too, is a very meaningful idea to Paul and is expressed in other places in his writings (Col. 1:10; 1 Thess. 2:12; Phil. 1:27). The calling which they have experienced is a call to come forth from the kind of life which they have known in their paganism and to live the kind of life which is worthy of the new religion which they have professed. In the Bible "to walk" means to live a certain kind of life. To walk in light is to live the good life; to walk in darkness is to live the bad life. To walk worthily of their calling means to live a life that will be worthy of the profession which they have made that Christ is their Lord, with the natural corollary that this makes all of them brothers in Christ, members of one spiritual family, parts of one spiritual body.

Verse 2, *with all lowliness of mind and meekness, with long-suffering, bearing with one another in love.* These are very specific terms qualifying the general idea in the previous expression "to walk worthily." The life that is lived in a manner worthy of the name "Christian" is one that is characterized by lowliness of mind, meekness, long-suffering, and forbearance in the broad, general area of love. It is interesting to observe that the word which is translated "lowliness of mind" was not used by the Greek people to describe a desirable characteristic at all. In the Greek literature outside of the New Testament a person who was marked by this characteristic—lowliness of mind or humility—would be looked upon as a weakling. It is not so in the Christian religion. The one who has come to know Christ and to experience the unmerited favor bestowed by God through Christ is marked by lowliness of mind rather than high-mindedness. This was another of the words which the Christians made to be a different word in their vocabulary, one with an exalted meaning.

In similar fashion, the term which is translated "meekness" must be understood in the light of its use by the Greek people rather than by the connotation which men put into it today. Just as lowliness of mind was not thought of as a desirable characteristic in Paul's day, so meekness is not generally considered a desirable characteristic in the twentieth century. The problem is one of English usage, by which meekness today does not at all mean what Paul's word meant. Meekness today is used to describe a spineless sort of person who may be pushed about by anyone a bit more aggressive. The word which Paul used, however, was a very strong and positive word. It had been used to describe a wild horse that had been tamed. The horse still had all of its old power and fire and determination, but these were yielded to the controlling hand of his master who held the reins. He was a "meek" horse. Meekness then meant surrendered power, obedient power. As Paul exhorted his readers to be meek, he exhorted them to yield to the controlling hand of their new Lord all the fire and power and determination that were in them. These are desirable qualities when they are dedicated qualities.

The word translated "long-suffering" means to bear long with the infirmities or the weaknesses of another. In general usage it described one who would bear long without striking back in revenge of personal injury or wrong. Such persons follow the character of God, who is spoken of as one who is long-suffering with men, that is, as one who bears long without striking out at men in vengeance. As the word is used in the New Testament it is closely related to the word "patience" and had a meaning which was more exalted than any which it had in non-Christian writings. The clause which follows, "forbearing one another in love," is for the purpose of explaining the word "long-suffering." In the all-encompassing area of Christian love the followers of Christ are to bear with one another in their weaknesses and in their difficulties as they try to live a life that is worthy of the calling which they have experienced.

Verse 3, *being speedy to keep the oneness which the Spirit produces in the bonds of peace*. This participle is variously translated "endeavoring," "eager," "giving diligence," etc. It is the Greek word from which we derive our English word "speed." It speaks of the burning eagerness or the blazing zeal by which one would carry out some proposed activity. Here that activity is the keeping of the unity or oneness which the Holy Spirit produces. The word translated "to keep" means to cherish or to guard carefully so as to keep or maintain. The present tense speaks of a continuous effort as well as of a present possession. Already they are in possession of this oneness, and they are to give diligent effort to maintaining the oneness. The word "Spirit" in the opinion of the best interpreters is a reference to the Holy Spirit. The Greek case is one which indicates that the Spirit is the active agent in producing the unity or the oneness. The Holy Spirit produces a state of unity among all true believers, and it is the responsibility of the believers to give diligent effort to the maintaining of that unity. The word "bond" is descriptive of a chain, and the word "peace" is in apposition with it. The Holy Spirit, according to Paul's metaphor, uses peace as a chain to bind together all the redeemed people of God and make them one. This oneness is further described in verses 4–6 in a series of seven separate "ones." The mass impact of the series of "ones" is most impressive, and the individual consideration of the "ones" continues and enlarges that impression.

Verses 4–6, *(There is) one body and one Spirit, even as you have been called also in one hope of your calling; one Lord, one faith, one baptism, one God and Father of all men, the one who is over all men and through all men and in all men.*

One Body

This entire statement appears to be an affirmation rather than an exhortation. If this is the case, we must understand a verb with an impersonal subject as we have translated it, "There is one body," etc. This "one body" is made up of all the redeemed. Many interpreters speak of this body as the church. Other interpreters object to the use of the term "church" with reference to this body because of the fact that predominantly in the New Testament the term "church" has reference to a local congregation. It is true that predominantly in the New Testament the term "church" refers to a local congregation, but it is doubtful that one can be true to the spirit of Paul in this passage without thinking of this one body of the redeemed in terms of "church." In Ephesians 1:22–23 Paul has already said that the exalted Christ has been made head "above all things in the church, which is his body." The relative pronoun "which" refers to church and is the qualitative relative, meaning the church *which is of such nature that* it is his body. Apparently Paul is enlarging the idea of church to include all the redeemed who make up the one body of which Christ is the head. It should be remembered that this idea of all the redeemed as one spiritual body with Christ as the head is never presented in the New Testament as an organized body. It is rather a metaphorical expression to describe a spiritual ideal. It is Paul's view that regardless of one's background culturally, racially, or otherwise, when he is redeemed he comes to be a part of the spiritual body of which Christ is the head.

One Spirit

The "one Spirit" which gives life to this one body is the Holy Spirit. Just as the human body has the animating spirit to give it life, so this one body has the animating Holy Spirit to give it life. He is the one who gives to it life and activity. He is the one who takes the twin chains of peace and love and uses them to bind together all the redeemed into one body. Very few interpreters have denied that this is a reference to the Holy Spirit. It is generally unquestioned that Paul is carrying forward his idea of the one body by seeing the one Holy Spirit as the energizing, life-giving, life-maintaining principle of this body.

One Hope

Even as you have been called also in one hope of your calling. There is one body, and there is one Spirit; in like fashion, there is one hope which characterizes this body. The one hope apparently means that all the redeemed hope for one and the same thing, that is, the ultimate consummation of all the redemptive purpose which God has promised them in Christ. They may have many desires and aspirations that differ; they have this one aspiration, this one hope, in common. This hope has its origin and basis in the calling which has been extended to them, which has brought them out of a life of heathenism and into a life redemptively related to God in Christ. When they were called out of that paganism, there was one hope planted within them, and that one hope they have in common with all other believers. It is a hope which is related to God's favor for sinful men.

One Lord

The "one Lord" named and obeyed by all those who make up this body is Christ himself. There is but one Lord. There can be but one Lord. The word which is used carries the idea of absolute lordship as it passes from one language to another. The Greek word *kurios* appears in the Latin as "Caesar," in the German as "Kaiser," and in the Russian as "Czar." These words bring automatically to the mind the concept which was latent in the Greek usage—one supreme Lord and Master. Jesus had taught the impossibility of man's being enslaved to two lords. There cannot be two lords; there can be only one Lord in the true sense of the word.

One Faith

There is "one faith" by which men come into relationship to Christ as Lord. Faith means trust. The faith which brought the Jew to an acceptance of Christ as Lord was the faith which brought the Gentiles to an acceptance of Christ as Lord. The faith which brought both to an acceptance of Christ as Lord is the same faith which has brought men in every age to such acceptance. There is one way and one only by which man comes into vital, saving relationship to God in Christ, and that is by way of faith. That was Paul's emphasis in Ephesians 2:1–10. It is his consistent emphasis at every point. There are not many "faiths" by which man comes to be related to Christ. There is but one faith, one trust by which that experience is realized.

One Baptism

Just as there is one faith by which all individuals come into saving relationship to Christ, there is "one baptism" by which they make outward demonstration of that inner spiritual experience. Baptism as it was used in the New Testament was a symbolic rite which pictured death to an old life and resurrection to a new life. The inner experience of faith stood at the beginning of the inner reality of one's relationship to Christ. The external act of baptism stood at the beginning of the external demonstration of that which one had experienced. The baptism which these Christians had experienced was one in its purpose—that of picturing or interpreting publicly one's experience of death and resurrection in their saving relationship to Christ. Those who trusted Christ in that day accepted baptism as a means of indicating that experience, even when it was unpopular to do so, even when it meant that they would be cut off from family and from friends, and, in many instances, when it meant that they would suffer persecution and even death. The one faith which they had in Christ was so precious to them that they desired that all men know that experience, and baptism was their way of demonstrating it.

One God and Father of All

Once again, simply, and without laboring to do so, Paul brings the Trinity into his discussion—one Lord, one Spirit, one God. There is one God, the God of Christian revelation, who is the Father of all those who have come to be a part of the spiritual body of which his Son Christ is the head. The word "all" in this passage appears to have specific reference to all the redeemed. It is not the idea of the universal fatherhood of God in the sense sometimes used that if there is one God he must be the Father of all men. Rather, the emphasis here is on the fact that there is one God and he is the Father of all the redeemed. There is a specific reference at this point: all those who have experienced this new spiritual life in relationship to his Son and have come to be a part of the one body of which his Son is the head have this one God as their Father. Again, without regard to previous cultural or racial lines they have one Father. There is a tremendous and awe-inspiring significance to this statement "Father of all," just as there is in Jesus' expression when in the Model Prayer he taught his followers to say, "Our Father." If one prays in the spirit in which Jesus taught us to pray, and if one thinks in the pattern of the inspired apostle at this point, he recognizes the truth that there is one God and Father of all the redeemed and in that sense all the redeemed are brothers in Christ.

Paul follows this statement with three prepositional phrases which are difficult to interpret. They may be another example of the multiplying of phrases to create the impression of the greatness of the one God and Father of all, or they may have separate force and significance. If the latter is true, the most likely interpretation is this: This one God is "over all" in the sense of his transcendence or sovereignty; he is "through all" in the sense of his pervading presence or immanence; he is "in all" in the sense of his constant indwelling presence through the Holy Spirit given to all believers. One stands in reverent awe as he looks at this idea of oneness—one body, one Spirit, one hope, one Lord, one faith, one baptism, one Father. How very much there is here to bind all believers together in the sense of oneness! At the same time one stands with head bowed in shameful confession of the failure of the Lord's people to carry out Paul's exhortation, "Be speedy to guard over carefully the oneness which the Spirit produces."

The Diversity Which Christ Provides, 4:7–11

Paul's concept of Christian relationship and service is always the concept of unity in diversity. This was true in his letter to the Corinthians (1 Cor. 12–14), in which he discussed many spiritual gifts for the benefit of the one body and the many members with their diversified functions within the one body. In this passage he carries out that same idea in more limited fashion.

Verse 7, *But to each one of us has been given the grace according to the measure of the free gift of Christ.* Here begins the idea of diversity. We are one body, but each member of that body is given a grace or a gift, a functional service to carry out. In the Corinthian passage Paul spoke of the different functions of the different members of the physical body (eyes, ears, hands, feet, etc.) as representing the idea of the different functions that must be carried out in the spiritual body of which Christ is the head. Not all members of the physical body of man perform the same function, and not all members of this spiritual body perform the same function. There are different functions given to individuals as a part of the sovereign bestowal of Christ. It is Paul's view that whatever gift one has he is to use to the utmost in his service to God.

In verse 8 Paul, in typical first-century Christian argument, finds a text in the Old Testament to demonstrate his point, *Having ascended unto the heights, he led captive captivity, he gave gifts to men.* This is a rather free use of

Psalm 68:18. It is one of many places in the New Testament where interpreters are inclined to become so involved in one part of the text quoted that they miss the main point which the writer had in mind. It must be recognized that from a textual viewpoint there are some problems involved in Paul's use. If one turns to read Psalm 68:18, he will find that Paul has not quoted the Psalm but has adapted it to his own use. The Hebrew of the text of the Psalm states, "Thou hast received gifts among men." Paul, however, quotes the passage, "He gave gifts to men." He changes the person from second to third, and he changes the verb from "receive" to "gave." He is not to be accused of erroneous quotation or of careless quotation. Certainly his quotation is deliberate because it is his reading of the passage as "he gave gifts," which carries out his idea at this point. He may have been following the custom of the Jewish teachers of his day to adapt a text from the Old Testament to illustrate a desired point. It is true, too, that there are versions of Psalm 68:18 (the Peshitta Syriac and the Chaldee Paraphrase) which have the reading "Thou didst give gifts to the children of men." The Hebrew verb which in Psalm 68:18 is translated "receive" is used several times in the Old Testament with the sense of bringing in order to give (Gen. 18:5; 27:13; 42:16; 48:9). It is also true that one of the Targums renders the passage "gave gifts to men." It appears clear that Paul is amply justified in using this reading of the Psalm to illustrate his idea of Christ's giving gifts to men. In Psalm 68 the conquering God (or the theocratic king, according to some interpretations) ascends his throne and receives men as captive gifts indicative of victory. In Ephesians 4 the conquering Christ ascends to heaven and distributes spiritual gifts to men for carrying out the work of his kingdom. It is a beautiful and forceful parallel.

In verses 9–10 Paul explains all that is involved in the expression "having ascended." When translated literally the passage is rather abrupt. The following is a literal translation and then a smoother paraphrase to indicate the meaning. *Moreover the "he ascended," what is it if not that he descended also into the lower parts of the earth? The one who descended, himself is the one who ascended also far above all the heavens, in order that he might fill the all things.* A bit more smoothly translated this will be the reading: *But this "he went up," what does it mean except that he also went down into the lower parts of the earth? The one who went down is the same one who went up also far above all the heavens, in order that he might fill all things.* Paul's explanation has given rise to a great variety of detailed and lengthy interpretations. The key to the problem appears to be in the term "the lower parts of the earth." There are three theories of interpretation which must be noted. For very comprehensive treatment of these theories the reader is referred to the rather technical discussions cited in the footnote below.[1]

What is meant by "the lower parts of the earth"? Some interpret the expression "the earth" to be in apposition with the term "the lower parts." This would mean that Christ descended from heaven to the lower parts of God's dominion, that is, the earth. This would have reference simply to the fact of his incarnation. He descended to the earth, and having finished his work, he ascended to heaven, and there

---

[1] S. D. F. Salmond, *The Epistle to the Ephesians* ("The Expositor's Greek Testament," Vol. III [Grand Rapids: Wm. B. Eerdmans Publishing Co., n.d.]), pp. 323–27; Lenski, *op. cit.*, pp. 517–25; Francis W. Beare, "The Epistle to the Ephesians," *The Interpreter's Bible*, Vol. 10 (Nashville: Abingdon-Cokesbury Press, 1953), pp. 687–89; Bo Reicke, *The Disobedient Spirits and Christian Baptism* (Kobenhavn: Ejnar Munksgaard, 1946), p. 233.

he dispenses gifts to be exercised by his workers on the earth.

Some understand the expression "the lower parts of the earth" to refer to the grave. They believe Paul to say that Jesus not only came down from heaven to the earth in his incarnation but that a part of the experience included his descending into the inside of the earth itself, that is, the grave. From the grave he was lifted up in his resurrection and ascended to heaven and there distributes gifts to men.

Still others understand the expression "the lower parts of the earth" to be a reference to the place of the departed dead, particularly the wicked dead. They understand Paul to say that Christ descended from heaven to the earth. When he was put to death at the end of his life on earth, he descended farther to the region of the dead, there either to proclaim his lordship over the wicked dead or (by some other interpreters) to release from death all of the saints who had died prior to that time. By this interpretation Christ descended to the region of the dead and led back to heaven all the saints who had died prior to his own death, so that the New Testament doctrine of the resurrection at the Second Coming of Christ would speak of the resurrection of believers who die between the time of the resurrection of Christ and the Second Coming.

There is neither the inclination nor the space to go into all of these theories at this point. Volumes have been written on the theories, and if the reader is inclined to pursue the study further, helpful direction will be found in the works cited in the footnote. To this writer the second of the two theories appears to be the most natural, the most reasonable, and the one most in line with the remainder of the New Testament teachings. From this viewpoint it appears that Paul is saying that the ascension of Christ implied a previous descent. He descended from heaven to earth in the experience of his incarnation for the purpose of redeeming man, which experience included death, burial, and resurrection.[2] Having carried out that work in the earth, he ascended to heaven, and there as the sovereign Lord he dispenses functions and responsibilities to be carried out by the workers whom he has left here in the world. This he did in order that he might complete all things relative to the redemptive purpose of God.

In verse 11 Paul indicates something of the variety of the gifts or functions which Christ has bestowed upon men: *And he himself gave some as apostles, some as prophets, some as evangelists, some as pastors and teachers.* Here is the diversity which Christ provides—a diversity of functional services in the spread of the good news of redemption for all men. Emphasis is placed upon the personal pronoun "he himself." It is this very Lord Christ who descended from heaven, carried out the redemptive work of God in the earth, and ascended to heaven to distribute these gifts.

These are representative services. In 1 Corinthians 12 another catalog of gifts is set out. Neither is to be thought of as exhaustive; both are representative, and both have definite backgrounds in the life of the people to whom Paul was writing. The apostles were those particularly sent with a message of redemption. The prophets were those who were spokesmen for God, giving evidence of speech under the direct movement of the Spirit. The evangelists were the ones whose responsibility it was to proclaim the good news of redemption. The last two words are so grouped grammatically that they appear to refer to one office rather than two—pastors and teachers. The word "pastor" was one which indicated the leadership of a group as a shepherd leads a flock;

[2] Compare this with the similar idea of humiliation and exaltation in Philippians 2:6–11.

and the word "teacher" was a word used for the one who instructed, particularly in doctrines. One function is then to be observed under the title "pastor and teacher." He is the leader of the flock, and he gives to them doctrinal instructions.

Apparently in the New Testament churches there were different persons for these many different functions. Just how sharply the line was drawn we cannot know definitely. We can know that in his sovereign wisdom Christ gave to men the responsibility and the ability to carry out his work, whether they served as apostles, prophets, evangelists, or pastors. In epistles of a later date (1 Tim.; Titus) other officers and services in the Christian group are recognized. The work of God has never been static. As new servants and services were needed, God led the people in the establishing of these offices and these functions. This diversity of service comes from the One who is himself the head of the body.

The Maturity Which Results from Both, 4:12–16

There is one body made up of many members. To these members Christ has distributed functional gifts that differ according to the needs of the work of God and perhaps, too, according to the nature of those who serve. Some have natural endowment or equipment for one kind of service and some for another. The diversity of function has, however, a unified end, and that is clearly and forcefully set out in verses 12–16.

Verse 12, *facing the equipment of the saints with reference to a work of ministry, looking to the building up of the body of Christ*. This indicates that all of these functional services point to one purpose, and that is the complete equipment of the saints for the work of Christ's service. In order that they shall be completely equipped for carrying out the service which he desired, they are given this distribution of functional services. All of these services in turn look to one end, and that is the building up of the body of Christ. They are not services that are to be performed with a view to honor involved or to self-interest enjoyed. They are rather services which are to be employed for the one constructive purpose of building or increasing, making to grow the body of Christ.

Verse 13, *until all of us attain unto the oneness of faith and full knowledge of the Son of God, unto a mature man, unto a measure of the stature of the fulness of Christ.* This giving of gifts in order that God's people will be completely equipped for the work of building up the body of Christ looks to the ultimate goal of spiritual development on the part of all, both individually and as a group. It is pointed to the goal of Christian attainment of such a oneness where faith and the full knowledge of the Son of God are concerned that they will be like a mature man or a full-grown man. The word which is commonly translated "perfect" does not mean simply sinless. It has to do with the idea of completeness or maturity. One grows until he attains the desired end for his growth. It is a word based on the same stem as the word which is translated "end." The end purpose of all the work of these many servants in this one body is the purpose of bringing the Lord's people as individuals or as a group unto the desired end of maturity or full growth.

That maturity or full growth is recognized in the closing phrase of verse 13, "unto a measure of the stature of the fulness of Christ." The goal for Christian growth as an individual or as a group venture is the approximation of the fulness of the stature of Jesus Christ. When one measures his growth or spiritual attainment by any other standard, he is using a standard that is too low. There is but one standard for the measurement of spiritual development as far as the New

Testament is concerned, and that is the fulness of the stature of Christ Jesus himself. If one would know the true nature of his spiritual growth or attainment, let him stretch himself up beside the fulness of the stature of Christ Jesus and look to see how much he lacks of approximating that stature. Until he attains to that desired end, that desired maturity, there is still something out ahead to beckon and to challenge to further growth. This further growth is to be realized in relationship to all of these services performed by the people of God.

Verses 14–16 form a long clause which is expressive of purpose both from the negative and the positive viewpoint. This purpose is related to the idea of Christian maturity to to the point of approximating the fulness of the stature of Christ. It is the goal for all believers, as will be seen in the subject of the verb in verse 13, "Until we, all of us, attain." Verse 14, *in order that no longer we may be babies, cloud-tossed and driven about by every doctrinal wind in the deceit of men, in craft facing the cunning of error.* The purpose of all these functional services is to bring the people of God to maturity so that they will no longer be as babies spiritually immature, persons who are tossed about like the clouds by every doctrinal wind that blows. As the clouds are tossed about by turbulent winds and blown one direction and then another by the wind, so some Christians as immature babies are driven helplessly before every doctrinal wind that blows. If the doctrinal wind blows in this direction, they are sent tumbling along ahead of it; if the doctrinal wind changes and blows in another direction, they in turn are sent tumbling along in that changed direction. This is an indication of spiritual immaturity and speaks of an absence of stability which ought to be a mark of one who has come to maturity in his Christian life.

Paul attributes these various doctrinal winds to the deceit which is practiced by men. The word translated "deceit" would be literally rendered into English by the word "cube." It is the Greek word for dice. As men are deceitful in their casting dice, so some men are deceitful in sending out doctrinal winds to blow the spiritually immature about like clouds. This deceitfulness of men is further modified by the expression "in craft facing the cunning (or method) of error." From the beginning of man's acquaintance with him, Satan has been recognized as one marked by deceit, craftiness, cunning, and error. It is he who motivates those men who are the agents of these doctrinal winds which blow the spiritually immature about. It is a mark of maturity when such craft and deceit are recognized and one is not blown along ahead of it.

Verses 15–16 in strong contrast give the positive purpose of this attainment to spiritual maturity: *but in order that, speaking the truth in love, we may grow with reference to all things unto him, who is the head, Christ, out of whom all the body (joined together and fitted together through every joint of supply according to the working in measure of each separate part) causes the increase of the body unto a building up of itself in love.* This is a passage of strong contrast. In contrast to the deceit of wicked men (v. 14), the Lord's people are to "speak truth in love." Deceit is to have no part in their life or in their practice. If their life is lived in the area of love and with love as its basis, this will be true of them.

Again, contrast is noted in the word "grow." Rather than being babies (v. 14), we will grow in every respect in our relationship to Christ. The expression "with reference to all things" speaks of Christian growth and maturity at every point. It is sad in life to see one who has grown physically but not mentally. The ideal is that one shall grow in every way that is normal for growth in human experience. So is it sad to see one who has grown normally from every physical standard but spiritually he is as immature as a baby. Christ gives all of these services looking to Christian growth at every point in relationship to him.

Again Paul comes to a central emphasis upon Christ as the head of the body. He is the head, and all the body stems from that head. The relative pronoun "whom" is in the ablative case, which speaks of source or origin. Out of Christ as the head stems all the body, and all this body, fitted together and joined together as is natural for a body, grows until it attains to the desired maturity. It is not the purpose of God that the body of which his Son Christ is the head shall be dwarfed. Rather, it is to be full grown. It is not the purpose of God that the body of which his Son Christ is the head shall be improperly fitted together. Building terms and musical terms are used together in verse 16. The term translated "joining together" is the basis for our English word "harmony." The term translated "fitted together" was used of a house or the parts of a musical score. The word which is translated "supply" was a musical term descriptive of the one who dispensed to the members of the Greek orchestra the sheet music and the other equipment which they would use. Each separate part of the body supplies that which is its natural purpose to supply, with the result that the body properly fitted and properly joined together grows as a normal body should grow. It is interesting that Paul speaks of this body as causing its own increase or making its own growth unto a building up of itself. It is the purpose of God that the body of Christ shall grow in every way that is fitting for such a spiritual body to grow, until it comes to full maturity and all of its life is exercised in the area of love.

IV

The Application of Redemption in Personal Life

(4:17 to 5:21)

One of the distinguishing features of the Christian religion is the way of personal life set out for those who are Christians. Nothing is more basic than this. Redemption in Christ means deliverance from the penalty and power of sin. While it means deliverance from the penalty of sin for the future in the sense of the individual's being saved for heaven and eternal fellowship for God, it also means deliverance from the controlling power of sin in this world, salvation to a new and victorious life here and now. If the religious experience with Christ professed by the individual does not correct the evil that was once in his life, either there is something wrong with the profession that the individual makes or there is something wrong with his own application of life and purpose to that profession. Throughout the New Testament the assurance is given over and over that the indwelling Christ has the power to change the complete life of the individual and make of him a new creation. It is necessary then to observe the significance of the application of redemption in the life of one who professes to have experienced it.

A New Philosophy of Life, 4:17–24

The redeemed person is to live a new life in the Spirit. The evil in the life of the Gentile world, the pagan world of Paul's day, was due to a false conception of the meaning of life. They thought life was just for the purpose of revelry in the indulgence of the appetites of the flesh. Paul's view is that the true conception of life is that lives are transformed by contact with Jesus Christ and, therefore, an entirely new product is seen—a new creation brought about by God through the renewing power of his grace.

The Gentile Philosophy of Life, 4:17–19

The dark picture of the Gentile way of life based on the Gentile philosophy of life is painted in verses 17–19. Paul begins the instruction with the statement that this way of life is not for the Christian, in verses 17–18, *Therefore, this I say and bear witness in the Lord, that you no longer walk about as the Gentiles walk about in the emptiness of their mind, being darkened in their understanding, being alienated from the life of God, on account of the ignorance which is in them, on account of the hardness of their heart.* In strong and impressive language Paul calls the Lord to be his authority as he bears witness to these Christians that they are no longer to walk about as once they walked about and as the Gentile world at large still walks about in the emptiness of their mind. There was a time when these Christians had been a part of that Gentile world and had shared the view of that world that life consisted of pleasure and the indulgence of the physical appetites. The present tense of the verbs used speaks of the fact that what was once a continuous conduct is no longer to be their conduct.

The expression "in the emptiness of their mind" is an impressive descriptive term which shows the reason for that Gentile conduct. The word translated "emptiness" means exactly that—the absence of any real content. The very thinking process of the Gentile world spoke of emptiness and nothingness as far as genuine values were concerned. This emptiness of mind is further described in verse 18. These Gentiles were darkened in their understanding and alienated from the transcendent life which is possible only for those who know the true God. They were darkened in their understanding and alienated from that life on account of the ignorance which was in them. This ignorance relates again to the emptiness of their thinking which led them to believe that life consisted of the indulgence of things material.

The expression "on account of the hardness of their heart" is variously interpreted. Some interpreters understand it to be related directly to the preceding expression "on account of the ignorance which is in them." If this is the correct interpretation, it means that the very ignorance in the mind of the Gentile was there because of the hardness of his heart. Other interpreters understand the expression to relate directly to the preceding participles, "being darkened" and "being alienated." If this is true, the phrase is merely an extension of the same idea, "they were darkened in their understanding on account of the ignorance which was in them, which ignorance consisted of the hardness of their heart." This latter view seems a bit more natural when one considers verse 19 and its relationship to that which has gone before.

Verse 19, *who are of such nature that being insensitive they have given themselves over to lasciviousness unto the working of all uncleanness in greediness.* The relative pronoun in this verse is qualitative and is always descriptive of character. These Gentiles, empty in their thinking, darkened in their understanding, alienated from the life of God because of ignorance of the true way of life, have in their insensitive spirits given themselves over completely to a life of lasciviousness and uncleanliness, all of which is practiced in the area of greed. So greedy are they for physical pleasures that they have given themselves over completely to the expression of the physical appetites, and they look upon that as being the highest good which life has to offer.

Such philosophy of life naturally results in the tragic moral and social conditions which characterized the Greco-Roman world in Paul's day. These conditions are reflected in the literature of the people of that day, and they are reflected in the ruins of the cities which were standing in that day. The moral and social conditions were unbelievably vile. Archeologists today, in digging out the ruins of some of those buried cities of Paul's day, have found it necessary to put covers over the ruins as they were uncovered because that which is depicted in stone and other art work would corrupt the very workers who were digging. It is to be kept in mind that in Paul's day those buildings were a part of the everyday life and experience of the people, looked upon not only by adults but by school children themselves. One who grows up in an atmosphere of that kind, taking that as the accepted way of life, can be expected to do nothing more than follow the way the mind is bent. Once these Christians had been a part of that paganism.

The Christian Philosophy of Life, 4:20–24

In these verses Paul shows in strong contrast the different sort of life and conduct for the Christian because of the different approach to life or philosophy of life which is his. *But you have not thus learned Christ, since indeed you have heard him and you have been taught in him just as truth is in Jesus, that you should put off according to your former way of life the old man who was corrupt according to the lusts of deceit, but to be renewed in the spirit of your mind, and to put on the new man, the one who has been created according to God in righteousness and holiness of the truth.* The pronoun subject "you" in verse 20 is emphatic. It is in contrast to the non-Christian Gentiles of verses 17–19. The strong adversative idea is that these who are Christians have learned a new philosophy of life, a new evaluation of and approach to life, as they have come to know Christ. The verb translated "learn" is the verb from which the word "disciple" is derived. They have come to know Christ in the role of disciples or learners. One of the vital things which they have learned is a new way of life and conduct. The conditional sentence in verse 21 does not raise a question; it affirms the fact that they have heard Christ and have been taught in him, just as truth is in him. This does not mean that they heard Christ himself. Rather, they heard Christ as he was preached to them by others who had come to know the truth in Christ. Jesus had referred to himself as the truth (John 14:6). He had said that he came into the world to bear witness concerning the truth (John 18:37). These Christians have been taught according to the truth that is in him and the truth which he brought into the world.

The content of that teaching concerning the true way of life in contrast to the false way of life of the Gentile world is given in verses 22–24. It consists of two things which are inseparable parts of one experience. First, they were to put off the former way of life which they had known before they came into contact with Christ and Christian truth. Second, they are to put on the new man, divinely created in righteousness and holiness which have their source in the truth. The illustration is a very graphic one. Missionaries from the

Orient report that it is a favorite illustration among the Oriental people because of the completely new way of life which they follow when they become Christians. Paul speaks of the experience as one in which they put from them the old man as one would put from himself a dirty robe. This old man was corrupt because of deceitful lusts which he had indulged. He had been deceived into believing that the proper approach to life was the indulgence of the physical desires or appetites. Such indulgence had been his "former way of life." Now that he has come to know Christ he has learned how erroneous was that former approach to life.

The same word that was used for "mind" in verse 17 is used for "mind" in verse 23. In verse 17 the Gentiles are pictured as walking about in the emptiness of their minds. In verse 23 the Christians are pictured as being renewed in (or by) the spirit of their mind. This speaks of a complete reversal in their way of thinking. Their way of thinking is new. Whereas once it dwelt upon emptiness, now it dwells upon those things which make for positive Christian living. The Christian life is one which is negative in that something is put out of the life or put off, but it is also positive in that something new replaces the old. So in verse 24 Paul says that a part of the lesson which these Christians have learned is the putting on of the new man who has been created according to God in righteousness and holiness which have their source in the truth. As one puts off an old soiled robe and puts on a new clean one, so the Christian in his experience turns from an old way of life, that of fleshly indulgence, to a new way of life, that in Christ.

The adjective translated "new" means new in kind. The life of the Christian is a new kind of life. The kind of life of the non-Christian Gentile was one molded by the emptiness of his thinking as he dwelt upon things physical. The kind of life of the Christian is new and different. It is one which is molded by the eternal God as he makes a new creation—a creation characterized by righteousness and holiness. It is an axiom of conduct that one's life depends upon his point of view. That axiom is nowhere better demonstrated than here. The Christian of the first century was indeed a new creation, and this new creation resulted from the redeeming and transforming experience which he had with Christ. This redeeming and transforming experience gave to him a new viewpoint, a new philosophy.

A Detailed Application of This Principle, 4:25–32

Verses 17–24 set out a fundamental principle of right living. Verses 25–32 set out a detailed application of this fundamental principle. While the former paragraph was general in nature, this one is specific in nature and follows the same approach by pointing up contrast between the old way of life and the new way of life. One is reminded of the teaching approach of Jesus in which he dwelt upon the negative only for the purpose of clearing the way for setting out positive truth and lines of positive conduct. Paul uses this technique most effectively at this point. He shows the error of the non-Christian way of life by speaking in negative terms to indicate that the Christian is to have no part in such conduct. Then in positive terms he presents that which is to be the conduct of the Christian, so that life for the Christian is not that of a vacuum from which all evil has been removed and there the process has stopped. Life for the Christian is something from which the evil has been removed, but the emptied space has been filled up by good, which not only fills up the space but overflows in blessing to others. This negative and positive approach to the Christian life is set out along five specific lines as follows.

Honesty Instead of Dishonesty, 4:25

This principle of conduct deals with basic honesty or integrity in one's relationship to his fellow man. The Jewish Christians had a background for this concept from their own religion and its injunction against bearing false witness. The Gentiles may have had some background for the concept of honesty. The life which they lived, however, indicates that if they had such a background it was very meager and of little influence. Paul holds up honesty as a basic element in Christian living. Verse 25, *Wherefore, having put off the lie, make a habit of speaking truth each one with his neighbor, because we are members of one another.* The negative statement is to the effect that lying is to be put aside once and for all. The tense of the verb speaks of a decisive, completed act, "having put off lying." On the other hand, the positive imperative is in the present tense, which has to do with continuous or habitual action, and so is rendered "make a habit of speaking truth." The dominating principle in the life of the individual is to be truth—honesty—in contrast with the dishonesty which once marked his life. This is to be true of every Christian.

The idea is presented in the use of the word "each." Each individual Christian is to make a positive habit of speaking the truth with his neighbor. The reason for this is observed in the causal clause which follows, "because we are members of one another." Apparently Paul is speaking here particularly of Christian relationship, and he goes back to his idea that we are all members of one body of which Christ is the head. Since we are all members of one body, we are to deal honestly one with the other. To exaggerate the figure a bit, one cannot conceive of the hand dealing falsely with the foot or the eye dealing falsely with the ear. So in the body of Christ each member is to deal honestly with his fellow member. This does not leave out honesty in relationship to those who are not a part of the body of Christ. It rather begins honesty at the proper starting point. Absolute honesty in all our relationship to those with whom we have most contact is just the starting point for honesty with all men as well.

Controlled Temper Instead of Excessive Wrath, 4:26–27

Another area where positive effort is to be employed to secure right living on the part of the Christian is the area of the control of one's temper. While it may not be easy to understand all that is involved in a part of Paul's instructions at this point, it is easy to understand the imperative which would indicate the avoidance of excessive wrath. Verses 26–27, *Be angry, and stop sinning; do not let the sun go down upon your wrath, neither give place to the devil.* Just exactly what does Paul mean when he says, "Be angry and sin not"? Perhaps some help is found in looking at the meaning of the word translated "be angry." It is a word which speaks of the revolt of mind against that which is unjust, shameful, or sinful. It is a word which speaks of fixed displeasure against that which is evil. The word is sometimes used of God's reaction, that is, his wrath, against what is evil. If this is the significance of the word, it is easy to see that there is a place for such attitude or emotion in the life of the Christian. The Christian is to have toward that which is evil the same fixed displeasure or revolt of mind which characterizes the Father God.

What then is meant by Paul's joining to this imperative another in striking negative fashion—"be angry and sin not"? The entire expression might be translated "be angry habitually and stop sinning." Perhaps this is Paul's warning that there is a certain danger involved in a person's exercising the attitude of wrath toward that which is evil, in the sense that this wrath may become resentment or exasperation to the point of sin itself. We speak often of righteous indignation. While we recognize that there is a proper place for such righteous indignation, we must recognize, too, that the Christian is never to let such attitude get out of hand. If such attitude comes to the expression of wrath, as it might be thought of in sudden flights of temper, it must be corrected at once. The Christian is not to sin by permitting even the correct attitude toward evil to become evil in its expression. Perhaps we do no violence to the thought of Paul if we paraphrase his expression to read, "Get hot, but cool off!"

The idea of bringing an end to the expression of wrath is further carried out in verses 26 and 27 when Paul indicates that the Christian is to let the anger of the day close with that day, that is, "stop letting the sun go down upon your wrath." In this expression the word "wrath" is a compound form. It is the basic word for wrath with a prepositional prefix, which makes it mean excessive wrath or a burst of wrath. If during the day the Christian has been guilty of such conduct, he is not to carry that experience on into the hours of darkness that are ahead. Perhaps Paul is thinking in terms of the Jewish view that the day ended with sundown and a new day started. The Christian is not to carry into a new day the exasperation which he has experienced today. Each day is to be sufficient within itself where such experience is concerned. Continuing this negative command, Paul says, "Stop giving place to the devil." Apparently he means that the Christian by excessive burst of anger gives to Satan a place in his life where Satan may find standing room to continue the evil in the heart of the individual. Never is the Christian to give Satan a working place in his life or a place where Satan may get a wrestling hold to bring the Christian to defeat.

Working and Giving Instead of Stealing, 4:28

Each of the detailed principles of conduct seems to be a bit more striking than the one which preceded it. Here Paul turns to one of the most beautiful concepts of Christian living, that is, that the proper approach to Christian living is not "What can I get?" but "What can I share?" Verse 28, *The one who steals let him steal no more, but rather let him labor, working with his own hands that which is good, in order that he may have something to share with the one who has need.* The Christian today may be a bit shocked when he reads Paul's instructions to Christian people, telling them to stop lying, to stop stealing, to stop many lines of conduct that are definitely not Christian. It must be remembered, however, that these were Christians who were just coming out of a life of paganism in which many of the things condemned from a Christian viewpoint were entirely acceptable. It must be remembered, too, that even after nearly two thousand years of Christian history it is still necessary for Christian ministers to proclaim from the pulpit to Christian people that honesty, integrity, and morality are Christian virtues and their opposites are to be left out of the Christian life.

In verse 28 Paul points to one who in the past had lived by the approach "What can I get from others?" To such extent had this been his practice of life that he had engaged in stealing the possessions of others. Now Paul indicates that such person is a Christian and is to stop taking the property of others. Here again he is not merely to stop stealing, thus putting out a negative and leaving a vacuum. Rather, he is to labor, working with his own hands at some honest trade, and this will have a good result along two lines. He will be supporting himself, and at the same time he will be making something which he can share with the one who is in need. This is the Christian approach to life—not taking from others that which belongs to them, but giving to others who are at the point of need. One is reminded of the viewpoint of Mrs. Wiggs of the cabbage patch on the occasion of the birthday party which her neighbors gave in her honor. Her first thought was that of sharing the refreshments with unfortunate neighbors who could not attend, because, as she expressed it, she never felt that anything which she had was really hers until she had shared it with someone else. So the Christians of Paul's day are encouraged in a positive outlook on life which will lead them to honest labor for the purpose of helping a needy neighbor.

Maintaining honest and gainful occupation meant much to Paul. He himself had engaged in his trade of tentmaking to provide his living expenses during a part of his missionary journeys. He had urged the Christians at Thessalonica (2 Thess. 3:10) to be busily employed in gainful occupation, even to the point of refusing to support people who would not work. In his letter to Titus (3:14) on the island of Crete he gave instructions that Christians were to maintain honest occupation. Hard work is always commendable in Christian living. It is doubly commendable when a person engages in it with the idea not only of supplying his own needs but of being able also to share with others who are in need.

Constructive Speech Instead of Destructive, 4:29

Another characteristic of the Christian in his personal life is that of constructive and pure speech in contrast to destructive and impure speech. Verse 29, *Every rotten word out of your mouth stop letting it go, but if any (word) is good facing the building up of need, in order that it may give grace to those who hear.* Once again there is the contrast of the negative and the positive. Negatively stated, the Christian is to stop letting any rotten word proceed from his mouth. The Christian's conversation is to be free of impurity and obscenity. There is an ancient proverb to the effect that the heart of man is a well and the mouth of man is a bucket and that which is in the well of the heart can be determined by what is in the bucket of the mouth. To one who has lived all his life with the conveniences of hot and cold running water that may not be a very meaningful proverb, but to one who spent the early years of his life in an environment where water had to be drawn up out of the well it is a most meaningful proverb. There were times when something came up in the bucket which was foreign material to the well! Then it was necessary to leave off the farm work while the well was cleaned out. So the proverb is most expressive—that which is in the heart of man can be determined even by the language which he uses. No foul word is to come forth from the mouth of the Christian, revealing the presence in his heart of that which is impure. The heart must be kept clean.

In beautiful contrast the positive side of Christian speech is indicated when Paul says that any word that is good for constructive purposes for building up at the point of need is to be spoken by the Christian in order that it may bring grace or blessing to those who hear him. There is no place in Christian speech for impure conversation. There is every place in Christian speech for pure conversation. Before a word is spoken or a story is told, let it pass the test "Is it constructive or destructive? Is it sound or rotten? pure or impure?" How often has the life of some immature Christian been cursed by the lingering memory of a rotten word or a foul story that had been told. Let such never be told by the Christian.

Unwillingness to Grieve the Holy Spirit, 4:30–32

The Holy Spirit is presented in the New Testament as a person, the third person of the Trinity. He is presented as the Spirit of God dwelling within the believer. The body is spoken of as the temple in which the Holy Spirit lives here in the world (1 Cor. 6:19–20). As a person, he may be grieved when materials foreign to the life of a Christian are brought in. Perhaps the foregoing practices when brought into the life of the believer within whom the Spirit dwells cause grief to him—that is, lying, wrath, stealing, corrupt speech. Perhaps those practices which follow in verse 31 are the practices which bring grief to the Holy Spirit when they are brought into the life of the Christian. Again, it may be that it is a total picture that is presented here and that all the practices in this paragraph from verses 25–32 are practices which grieve the Holy Spirit.

Verse 30, *And stop grieving the Holy Spirit of God, in whom you have been sealed unto redemption day.* Here again is the present imperative with a negative particle to prohibit the continuance of action already in progress. Whatever the immediate reference, whether to the practices already discussed or those to be discussed in verse 31, they are practices which have been in the life of those who are now believers, and they are to be stopped. Their continuance will mean the continuance of grief to the indwelling Spirit in whom believers have been sealed, looking to the day of the redemption of the body in the resurrection. The body which is to be redeemed in the experience of the resurrection, the body which is the dwelling place of the Holy Spirit here in this world, is not to be corrupted by these evil practices.

Verse 31, *All bitterness and anger and wrath and clamor and reviling, let it be put from you along with all malice.* These are practices which speak of the sins of the spirit or the sins of the disposition. Whereas corrupt speech, stealing, and lying may be expressions of the sins of the flesh, these (bitterness, excessive anger, clamor, reviling, and malice) are the sins of the disposition or of the spirit. They cause as much grief to the indwelling Spirit as do sins of the flesh. Perhaps Christians have not been as diligent as they should have been in pointing out the evils of the sins of the disposition. Often one is heard to speak or to preach denouncing the gross sins of drunkenness, immorality, stealing, murder, and such. Having denounced these sins, he may feel that he has shown real courage. That, however, is questionable. It is entirely possible that the greater percentage of his listeners are in agreement with him when he denounces these sins of the flesh. Let him, however, come to denounce the sins of the spirit—strife, bitterness, malice, injustice, prejudice—and he may find that the percentage is reversed and that more courage is required to denounce the sins of the disposition than to denounce the sins of the flesh. They go together, and both of them grieve the indwelling Spirit of God.

Verse 32, *but become with reference to one another kind, compassionate, forgiving each other just as God also in Christ has forgiven you.* Here Paul brings another contrast between the positive and the negative. Bitterness, malice, and such things are to be put away from the believer. Instead of being marked by such conduct, believers are to become kind in their relationship one to the other. The word which is translated "kind" means the exercise of thoughtful consideration. In the midst of all the life situations which might produce strife and bitterness Christians are to exercise thoughtful consideration one for the other.

A story which has been told so long that likely its origin has been lost is a good illustration at this point. The story is that of a class of boys and girls in which an examination was being given in art appreciation. One little fellow received the painting *Spirit of '76* as the art object concerning which he was to write an essay. It will be recalled that this is a painting from the period of the American Revolution, and in the painting three soldiers are marching along together, one with a drum, one with a fife, and the third with a bandage about his wounded head. A part of the very discerning essay of the little boy was this: "*Spirit of '76* is a painting of three men. One of them is beating a drum; one of them is blowing a horn; and the other one has a headache!" This is a day when there is much of drumbeating, much of hornblowing, and many people have headaches. In such a situation what is to be the conduct of the Christian? He is to exercise thoughtful consideration.

Another characteristic of the Christian is that of compassion, "become compassionate unto one another." This is expressive of the deepest concern and feeling for our fellow man in his need. Christians follow in the footsteps of their Lord Christ. When he was here in the world, he was often moved with compassion as he looked upon people in their needs. The Christian is to become increasingly like him at that point. To look upon men in their need is to share sympathetically with them at the point of their need and, as far as it is humanly possible, to carry a part of their burden in our own hearts.

Again, Paul says that Christians are to exercise forgiveness in their relationship one to the other, and a comparative clause follows indicating that Christians are to forgive one another after the manner of God's forgiveness extended to us. God has in Christ forgiven us. He had so much more to forgive in us than we have to forgive in one another that we cannot as his children refuse to exercise that same attitude of forgiveness. At the same time, appreciation of the love and forgiveness which God has shown us in Christ should cause us to turn from every type of evil conduct, such as that which Paul has described in this paragraph as having no place in the life of the Christian.

Walk in Love, 5:1–5

Verse 1, *Therefore become mimics of God, as beloved children.* Paul's favorite word for bridging two ideas or relating one idea to another is repeated here, "therefore." It goes back to the passage immediately preceding it—the idea of the Christian's exercise of forgiveness following the pattern of God's exercise of forgiveness. The Christian is in every way to imitate God. That is the word that is used, "become imitators of God," or, to transliterate the expression, "become mimics of God." Again a comparative phrase is added, "as beloved children." Just as children imitate the father whom they love, so Christians are to imitate the Father whom they love, that is, God. It is a trait of the conduct of children that they have a way of imitating the father that they love and admire. They want to be like him. This is a commendable quality for Christians. As they look to the Father God, they are to imitate him; they are to want to be like him.

Verse 2, *and keep on walking about in love, just as Christ also loved us and gave himself in behalf of us, an offering and sacrifice to God unto an odor of sweetness.* A part of this imitation of the divine conduct is to be that of walking about in love. Paul's favorite verb "walk about" is joined to another favorite concept, "love," and the two together describe the total of Christian conduct. Love is to be the all-comprehensive area in which a child of God is to walk about. The model of this exercise in the area of love is to be the conduct of Christ. He loved us to the extent that he gave himself in sacrificial death for us. He loved us to the extent that he gave up his own best interest in order that the best interest of those who were the objects of his love might be carried out. This is to be the pattern for the Christian's exercise of love; his total life is to be described as one which is carried out by the practice of walking in love.

Again, in verses 3–5 Paul sets out several lines of conduct which are to have no part in the Christian life and which cannot be considered as a part of the life of one who is walking in love. His total purpose is that of an appeal that these Christians shall be altogether separate from those practices which mark their neighbors, the Gentiles. Verses 3–4, *But fornication and all uncleanness or covetousness, let it not be named among you as becoming to saints, and filthiness and foolish talking or idle jesting, which things are not fitting, but rather thanksgiving.* Here Paul lists a number of evil practices which have no part in the Christian life, but which were practices quite common in the non-Christian Gentile world. "Fornication and all uncleanness" seem to be comprehensive in their reference to moral purity. The word "covetousness" is descriptive of greed which causes one to yearn for that which is not rightfully his, perhaps even to the extent of being dishonest in order that he might obtain that which he covets. Paul says that such practices are not even to be mentioned as fitting conduct for saints. The word "saint" means very exactly one who is set apart. In the New Testament it is a synonym for believer or Christian. These practices are so vile that they are not even to be named as possible practices for believers.

Joined to these words are others which speak of similar

evil practices. In verse 4 the word translated "filthiness" was used in relationship to moral uncleanness as well as in relationship to matters of dishonesty. The words translated "foolish talk" and "idle jesting" would be parallel to the idea of "rotten words" in verse 29 of chapter 4. Paul does not condemn here the display of clean and wholesome humor. He himself on occasions used such. He speaks of the kind of idle chatter and low jesting which within themselves are blameworthy. These, he says, are not fitting where Christian speech and conversation are concerned, and he suggests a positive alternate in his term "but rather thanksgiving." This is one of the words for prayer in the New Testament. It is a word used for prayer as the expression of gratitude for all the favor which God has bestowed. Paul suggests that the speech of the Christian be characterized by thanksgiving, by positive traits rather than by these negative qualities that are not fitting for the Christian.

Verse 5, *For this you know full well that every fornicator or unclean person or covetous person (which is idolatry) has not an inheritance in the kingdom of Christ and God.* Paul in this expression indicates the reason that the foregoing conduct has no place in the life of the Christian. It is for the simple reason that such is the conduct of one who is not a part of Christ's kingdom at all. A very strong expression is used in the beginning of the verse, "knowing you know" or "you know full well." He indicates that one who is living a life of immorality or a life dominated by covetousness is by that very life indicating that he is not a part of Christ's kingdom.

It is instructive to observe that Paul equates covetousness with idol worship. Reading the Scriptures can sometimes produce a rather uncomfortable sensation because they condemn one's sin. There is one place where that is not true, and that is Exodus 20:3, "Thou shalt have no other gods before me." One reads that passage, breathes a sigh of relief, and says, "Well, at least that is one Commandment that I do not break. I am not an idol worshiper." Can one be so sure that he is not an idol worshiper, however, in the light of Paul's interpretation? Whatever a person wants to the extent that it comes to have first place in his heart—a place which belongs to God alone—comes to be his god. He is giving to it the devotion which is due to God alone. All of such conduct speaks of one who has not come to know the kingdom of Christ, the kingdom in which Christ reigns as supreme Lord. To walk in the midst of such conduct as is here described is not to walk in love, which Paul holds to be the Christian walk.

Walk in Light, 5:6–14

One major concept or figure of speech follows another as Paul makes application of the truth of redemption in the area of the Christian's personal life. Having spoken of the responsibility of the Christian to walk in love, he turns now to a slightly different but definitely related idea, and that is that the Christian is to walk in light. This means to walk the way of one who is enlightened to know the truth of God and what God desires for his people.

Verse 6, *Let no one deceive you with empty words, for on account of these things the wrath of God comes upon the sons of disobedience.* To Paul's mind, empty words would be words suggesting that the line of conduct set out in verses 3–5 were acceptable for Christian practice. He urges his readers not to be deceived by such empty talk and assures them that these very practices bring the displeasure of God upon those who are characterized by disobedience. In his holiness God cannot be pleased with evil practices. These evil practices can result in nothing short of the outpouring of the displeasure of God upon those who follow them.

Verses 7–8, *Therefore, become not their partners, for you were once darkness, but now (you are) light in the Lord, walk about as children of light.* The word "therefore" relates to the coming of wrath upon those who practice evil. The Christians are not to become partners in evil practice with those who are described as sons of disobedience. The word translated "partners" is an adjective meaning "sharers with." Christians are not to share with the sons of disobedience in their evil practices. Perhaps Paul is suggesting that to share with them in their evil practices would mean to share with them in the displeasure of God. He reminds them in verse 8 that once they lived in the dense darkness of their paganism but now they know the light of God. Just as once they walked about in that darkness, so now they are to walk about as children who are characterized by the light, that is, as children who know the light of God, the way of God. This is a similar idea to that which he set out in 2:1–10—once they walked about in trespasses and sin, but now they are to walk about in good works.

In verse 9 Paul speaks of the fruit which is produced by this life of walking in light. *For the fruit of the life (is) in all goodness and righteousness and truth.* The life of one who walks in the light of God bears fruit for God in the areas of goodness, righteousness, and truth rather than in the areas of the wicked practices of the previous discussion.

In verses 10–11 Paul takes up the imperative of verse 8, *as children of light walk about . . . proving what is well-pleasing to the Lord, and not having fellowship with the unfruitful works of darkness, but rather exposing them.* The participle in verse 10 means to examine or to investigate as to genuineness. As the Christians walk in light they demonstrate the genuineness of all that is well-pleasing to the Lord rather than that which would bring about his displeasure. As negatively stated in verse 11, the believers are to have nothing in common with the unfruitful works of darkness. The term translated "stop having fellowship" means very exactly "stop having anything in common with." The Christian life is to have nothing by way of common interest, common purpose, or common plan with the unfruitful works of darkness, that is, the works of evil. Rather, by walking in the light the believers are to rebuke these works of darkness and expose them for what they really are. The word in verse 10 translated "proving" or "demonstrating" was used for testing coins to determine genuineness. By walking in the light, the Christian demonstrates the genuineness of those things which please God and the counterfeit nature of all evil practices.

Verses 12–13, *For the things which are being done secretly by them it is shameful even to mention; but all things being rebuked by the light are made manifest, for everything which is made manifest is light.* Here Paul speaks of the evil practices which are carried on, in a manner of speaking, under cover of darkness, carried on in secret. These are practices which are too shameful even to mention. To know the practices of the Roman world is to understand something of the unspeakable evils concerning which Paul is writing. He gives assurance, however, that all these evil practices are to be rebuked by the light of God. It is the very light of God's revelation played upon them which brings them out into the open so their true nature is revealed. Every evil practice is shown up in its true nature when the light of God is brought to bear upon it. It is a part of the Christian's responsibility to live in such a way that he will bring this light of God to bear upon all evil.

In verse 14 Paul gives expression to a demonstration of this truth from the viewpoint of the Old Testament: *Wherefore it says, Arise, oh sleeping one; stand up from among the dead ones, and Christ will shine upon you.* Those who have slept in the night of the darkness of evil, those who have been dead in the midst of evil practices, are called upon to arise from their sleep, to stand up from their dead position, and to experience the full light which Christ will turn upon them. As people who live a new life, they are to walk in that light of Christ.

Walk in Wisdom, 5:15–21

Another approach to the problem of the right kind of life for the redeemed is that of walking in wisdom. This is closely related to that of walking in love and walking in light. Here the particular point of interest is that which has to do with living a life which is based on the right choice. Verses 15–17: *Therefore, make a habit of watching carefully how you are walking about, not as unwise ones, but as wise ones, redeeming the time, because the days are evil. On account of this stop becoming foolish, but make a habit of understanding what the will of the Lord is.* The light of Christ has been focused upon the path which he would have his followers to walk. They are to watch carefully how they walk. The present imperative justifies the translation "make a habit of watching." They are to be alert at all times to the way that they walk, not in the manner of unwise people, but in the manner of wise people. The word which is translated "wise" is a very forceful construction. It meant the ability to make the right choice. When one is faced by multiple choices at the point of conduct, it is extremely important that he make the right choice. It is particularly important that believers make the right choice, because, as Paul expresses it, "the days are evil." They lived in evil days. Those were days when evil practice was the accepted pattern of life. In such a day it was most important that a Christian make the right choice as to what his life was to be.

In verse 16 the word translated "redeemed" was a market term for being alert to seize an opportunity at a bargain. It was a word which every reader of the epistle would understand. By it Paul was saying, "Be alert in these evil days to seize the opportunity at making the right choice." In verse 17 he carries on this same emphasis. Because they lived in evil days, they were not to become foolish, that is, making the unwise choice. They were to understand at all times what was the Lord's will for them. The term translated "will" is the one previously discussed which meant basically "the Lord's wish." When the believer faces multiple choices at the point of the line of conduct, he is to make his decision on the basis of his understanding of what the Lord wishes for him to do and what will be the right choice in that circumstance. In the verses that are to follow Paul sets out two lines of conduct. The believer, as he walks in wisdom, is to choose the proper line of conduct according to that which the Lord would wish for him.

Paul speaks first of conduct which is physically stimulated and which results in riotousness. Verse 18, *And be not drunk with wine, in which is riotousness.* Here is a line of conduct which results in unusual activity. It is a line of conduct which is produced by the stimulant of strong drink. The result of that line of conduct is riotousness or dissoluteness. That is one choice that is held out before man, but is it the wise choice? Is it the choice which will be pleasing to the Lord? Is it the choice which will give a person the consciousness that he is doing that which the Lord desires in any given circumstance?

In contrast Paul presents another line of conduct, which is stimulated by the Holy Spirit and which results in a life of praise and worship. Verses 18–21, *but be filled with the Spirit, speaking to one another in psalms and hymns and spiritual songs, praising and singing in your heart to the Lord, giving thanks always on behalf of all in the name of our Lord Jesus Christ to God even the Father, subjecting yourselves to one another in reverence for Christ.* This passage may reflect the idea that was expressed at Pentecost. When the apostles were stimulated by the Holy Spirit, they carried on in a most unusual way, preaching the gospel in languages that could be understood by Jews who had come to Jerusalem from every part of the Roman world. In the midst of all of the excitement, when a question was asked as to an explanation for this unusual conduct, some of the Jewish leaders scoffed and said that this unusual conduct was due to the fact that the apostles were drunk. Peter, however, had a different explanation. He said that this was unusual conduct which could be explained only on the basis of the Holy Spirit's pouring out his power in order that his people might witness for him (Acts 2:1–21).

Now Paul contrasts two lines of conduct: one physically stimulated by wine, resulting in evil living; one spiritually stimulated by the Holy Spirit, resulting in a life of praise to God. Which is the wise choice? Which is the choice that will be in line with the will of the Lord? It is abundantly clear that the redeemed person, as he looks carefully to the way of his walk, will choose not the line of conduct physically stimulated, resulting in riotousness but rather the line of conduct spiritually stimulated, resulting in worship.

Paul speaks here in terms of worship, as he indicates that the Christian worship is carried out as an expression of praise and thanksgiving in song. Three different types of songs are here described. Apparently all of these musical forms were used in the worship service of the early church.

The word translated "psalms" is the word for the psalms which appear in the Old Testament. This was the songbook of the Hebrew religion. The word is based on a verb which originally meant "to stroke" and was related to the playing of a stringed instrument. The word "psalm" came to be used for a song which was sung to an instrumental accompaniment. It is quite certain that in the early churches they used the Old Testament psalms as a part of their worship form. The psalms would be most fitting because of their background in Jewish usage and because of the beautiful way in which they register every emotion of the heart as one comes to worship.

"Hymns" was a word used for songs of praise to the divine Person. Augustine, who made a very careful study of the services of the early church, insisted that hymns had to include three elements: a hymn had to be a song of praise; it had to be addressed to God; it had to be sung. Unless it involved all three of these elements, he insisted it was not a hymn. Clearly set out in the New Testament are traces of many of the hymns of the early churches: Luke 1:46–55, 68–79; Acts 4:24; Ephesians 5:14; Philippians 2:6–11; 2 Timothy 2:11–14; 1 Timothy 3:16. Perhaps the one which is most fully set out is this last one in 1 Timothy 3:16.

> He who was manifest in the flesh,
> Justified in the spirit,
> Seen by angels,
> Proclaimed among the Gentiles,
> Believed in the world,
> Received up in glory.

This is a hymn on the incarnation of Christ, and likely it was based on a very early creedal statement. In the first two lines one sees the *fact of the incarnation;* in the second couplet (lines 3 and 4) he sees the *manifestation of the incarnation;* in the third couplet (lines 5 and 6) he sees the *result of the incarnation.* It is a beautiful hymn, even more beautiful when one reads it in the balanced cadence of the Greek text.

"Songs" is the word from which we get our English word "ode"—spiritual odes or poems. These were apparently songs that were more subjective in nature, telling of religious experience or perhaps telling the story of some religious hero. In our own musical expression of religious devotion we have followed all three of these patterns. In some instances, though regrettably in too few instances, we still sing the Old Testament songs. We have our own hymns which are objective in their nature as they give praise and expression of adoration and devotion; likewise, we have our spiritual songs to interpret our own subjective religious experiences as well as those of other Christians. All of this is an outgrowth of the Spirit's working within us. The natural result of that working within is a life that goes up to God in an expression of adoration, praise, and thanksgiving.

Paul closes the discussion by saying that in all this we are subject ourselves one to the other in reverence for Christ. This looks backward to all that he has said about the application of redemption in the personal life of the believer. We live our lives in a social framework in relationship one to the other, and that involves the idea of mutual submission one to the other as we walk in love, in light, and in wisdom. This mutual subjection one to the other is carried out in the spirit of reverence which Christ produces within. When the believer stops to consider *what once he was* and *what now he is* as a result of God's redemptive work within him, it creates an attitude of awe and wonder which must dominate the entire thought and life of the one who belongs to Christ.

V

The Application of Redemption in Domestic Life

(*5:22 to 6:9*)

The last area to which Paul applies the practical phase of redemption is domestic life. This, too, is one of the basic elements in the Christian religion. The effects of redemption in Christ do not stop in the life of the individual. They carry over into every relationship of that life—in society, in the church, and in the home. It is perhaps in the home that real Christianity meets its most severe test. Ideally this should not be true, but practically it appears to be true. What is the nature of one's expression of his religion when the curious and prying eyes of public opinion have been shut out by the walls of the home and the individual expresses himself only in relationship to that little private circle? Here is one of the real tests of life and of religion. A fellow minister has a way of saying in apparent humor and yet in genuine seriousness, "Any man can be nice to his secretary; God wants us to be nice to our wives!"

It is interesting to observe that the instruction which we have here concerning the application of Christianity in the home comes from one who was not himself a married man.

Whether or not Paul had ever been married will probably always remain a question to vex the minds of interpreters. Certainly when he wrote 1 Corinthians 7:7 (a few years before he wrote Ephesians), he was not married.

Paul had a good background for writing with reference to the home. His childhood home was one that was devoutly religious. This appears to be clear from Philippians 3:4–6 and 2 Corinthians 11:22. We do not know whether or not Paul's family ever embraced Christianity. Some of his family may have embraced Christianity. At least, he had a nephew in Jerusalem who helped him when there was a plot on the part of the Jewish religious leaders to put Paul to death before he could have legal trial (Acts 23:16). It would seem unlikely that this nephew would have helped Paul apart from sympathy with him as a Christian. Whether or not the family embraced Christianity, it had afforded for Paul the right kind of religious atmosphere to prepare him for the life that was to be his, first as a Jewish rabbi and then as a Christian missionary. Paul had also the teachings of Jesus and Jesus' appreciation for women and children to give additional background for his views of the home.

It is scarcely possible to conceive of a nobler view of marriage and the home than that which appears in this passage in Ephesians. The Christian world today needs to take this whole passage in a serious attitude. There is far too much trouble today between husbands and wives, between parents and children, between masters and servants. All these areas of domestic life can be greatly improved if all parties involved approach the problems of mutual interest from a Christian viewpoint. It may well be noted that apparently the starting place for this emphasis is in the pulpit. Our decaying domestic situation is not going to be improved until a higher standard for marriage and the home is held up in the pulpit. That higher standard is not going to be held up until ministers and teachers return to serious consideration of the teachings of the New Testament relative to marriage and the home.

Duty of Wife to Husband, 5:22–24

In this passage Paul writes of three areas of mutual Christian responsibility in the home. The first is the area of the mutual responsibility of husband and wife. He begins, as any good teacher with a Jewish background would naturally begin, with the responsibility of the wife to her husband. It is necessary to understand a verb form of some kind in verse 22. Some interpreters understand the same participle which appeared in verse 21, that is, "subjecting themselves" or "being in subjection." Other interpreters accept the same verb for being in subjection but feel that the verb form should be imperative since it is an imperative which is used at every other point in this general passage: 5:25; 6:1, 4–5, 9. In either construction the verb will have the force of an imperative. In Greek when a participle is joined to an imperative, it takes on the force of an imperative. The use of the third person possessive pronoun inclines one to the view that the form which is to be understood here is the participle. This custom of the Greek language to understand such a participle to have the force of an imperative assures us that it is that emphasis which Paul desires to make.

Verse 22, *Wives subjecting themselves to their own husbands as unto the Lord.* If we render the form with the force of an imperative it would be, *Wives, subject yourselves unto your own husbands as unto the Lord.* The force is the same. It will be observed by those who are acquainted with the Greek text that there is an unusual construction here in that the word "wives" is apparently in the vocative case, and yet it has the definite article with it, "the wives." The same pattern appears in Paul's instruction to husbands (5:25), to children (6:1), to fathers (6:4), to servants (6:5), and to masters (6:9). This is most likely what is known as the generic use of the article. In such usage the article binds all of the individual members into one class. It is a comprehensive statement, indicating that the responsibility is one which is for all wives. The verb "be in subjection to" is a military term descriptive of the exercise of the proper spirit of subordination of an inferior to a superior officer. Literally, it means "to line up under." Wives are enjoined by Paul to subordinate themselves to their husbands in a manner becoming their position as wives.

Interpreters differ in their understanding of the expression "as unto the Lord." Some understand this to be Paul's way of saying that it is the Christian duty of the wife to subordinate herself to her husband. That may be true. On the other hand, however, it is possible to understand this as a comparative expression, speaking of mode or manner. Why does one subordinate himself to the Lord? Because he finds the Lord to be worthy of that trust or subordination. Why is the wife to subordinate herself to her husband? Because she finds him one who is worthy of that trust or subordination. If this is the correct interpretation, we must remember that Paul is dealing with the ideal situation. In verses 25–31 he is going to set out the duty of the husband to the wife. If the husband will exercise himself in his relationship to his wife after the manner of Paul's instruction, he will be a husband worthy of the trust and the subordination which his wife exercises.

Verse 23, *because a man is head of the woman as Christ also (is head) of the church, himself Saviour of the body.* In stating that the man is head of the woman Paul is simply stating that which was accepted and universally recognized as being correct. In 1 Corinthians 11:3 Paul had given his idea of the order of rank in the Christian system: God, Christ, man, woman. It is that same idea which he expresses here. As in the creation story man came before woman, so it was understood in the matter of rank that man was superior to woman.

This was not only a recognized idea in the Jewish world but also in the Gentile world; man was head of the woman. In 1 Peter 3:7 Peter, in giving instruction to husbands in relationship to their wives, urged them to dwell with their wives according to the knowledge that while the woman was the weaker vessel she was man's equal at the spiritual level. It apparently solves nothing for one to say: "Oh, they were living in a different day than ours. If Paul and Peter were living today, they would not take the position that man was head of the woman." Such viewpoint is, of course, entirely conjectural. When one reads all the writings of these men in the New Testament, he is quite hesitant to make such a statement as that. Most likely, if they were living today, they would take exactly the same position. This is not to disparage the place of woman. The privileges which women enjoy today can, for the most part, be attributed to the emphasis on freedom and equality which is found in the Christian religion. The woman did not have equality even among the Jewish people until the principle of freedom was established by Christianity.

Paul illustrates the relationship of husband as head of the wife by using Christ and his relationship to the church. Christ is the head of the church. After this same pattern, the husband is head of the wife. Christ has the best interest of the church at heart. He is himself the Saviour of the body. In verse 25 Paul will instruct the husbands that they are to have the best interest of their wives at heart, too. It is such mutual relationship of husband and wife which is presented as the Christian approach to marriage.

Verse 24, *But as the church subjects itself (or is subjected) to Christ, thus wives also to the husband in everything.* The wife is to subject herself or subordinate herself to the husband in every way, just as the church subjects or subordinates itself to Christ. Mention perhaps should be made again of the idea in verse 22. The church subjects itself to Christ because it finds him worthy of, and properly responsive to, that subjection. The wife subjects herself to the husband in the same way because she finds him worthy of, and properly responsive to, such subjection. This is the Christian ideal.

Duty of Husband to Wife, 5:25–33

Continuing the discussion of marriage as a matter of mutual responsibilities and reactions, Paul takes up specifically the duty of the husband in his relationship to the wife. This has already been introduced in verses 22–24. Here it is specifically discussed.

Verse 25, *Husbands, love your wives, just as Christ also loved the church and gave himself in behalf of it.* Again the generic use of the article appears. All husbands are, by this construction, included in the imperative. The present tense of the imperative speaks of habitual or continuous action, "Husbands, keep on loving your wives," or, "Husbands, make a habit of loving your wives." The love of the husband for the wife is to be the continuous, abiding, habitual emotion. It is not to be interrupted by things (whether little or big) which might conceivably interrupt such attitude or emotion. When the husband made his vow, "For better or for worse, till death do us part," he meant just exactly that. The verb that is used for love is the very strong *agapaō*. It is the word which speaks of supreme evaluation. It is the word which is used in John 3:16 to speak of God's love for the world. God put such value upon the world that he would not leave it in its sin, even when it cost his only begotten Son as the price of redemption. Man puts supreme evaluation upon his wife —such evaluation that he will not let that relationship go in the face of difficulties, whether small or great.

Paul repeats the analogy of Christ's relationship to the church and uses it as the manner of the husband's love for the wife. The husband is to keep on loving his wife "just as Christ also loved the church, and gave himself up for it." Christ's relationship to the church is very graphically presented in the aorist tense, which brings all that he did for the church together and presents it as one supreme act of love. He loved the church and gave himself up for it. This means that he loved the church to the extent that he gave up his own best interest out of consideration for the best interest of the church. Christ did not conduct his life in answer to the question "What is to my best interest?" He conducted his life in answer to the question "What is the best interest of the church?" If he had conducted his life according to his own best interest, there would have been no Gethsemane, no Gabbatha, no Golgotha. He gave up his own best interest and experienced the agony of Gethsemane, the agony of mistreatment at the time of his trial, and the agony of the cross. This is to be the standard by which a man judges his love for his wife. He is to love his wife to the extent that he will give up his own best interest in order that the best interest of the wife shall be advanced. If husbands were more diligent in practicing the imperative of verse 25, is it not likely that wives would more readily practice the imperative of verse 22?

Verses 26–27, *that he might sanctify it, having cleansed*

(it) by the washing of water in the word, in order that he himself might present to himself the church glorious, not having spot or wrinkle or any such thing, but in order that it might be holy and spotless. This passage suggests a second word to indicate a man's relationship to his wife, and that is the word "cherish." It will be used specifically in verse 29, but it is in the background of this passage as well. Christ gave himself up for the church in order that he might set the church apart as a dedicated, cleansed, and glorious body. Interpreters at times have wrestled in embarrassment with this passage in trying to relate it in some way to the customary bath which the bride took in that day as a part of the marriage ceremonial. They have had difficulty with it because so to understand it would suggest the idea of Christ's giving the bath to the church, which is his bride. It is very unlikely that that is in Paul's mind at this point. He speaks of the work of Christ in the interest of the church in sanctifying it (setting it apart as holy), in giving it spiritual cleansing in relationship to his word, and in thus preparing for himself a glorious bride, free from any spot or wrinkle. The word translated "spot" means impurity. The word translated "wrinkle" means sign of decay or age. Christ acted in such way in relationship to the church that he assured for himself the most desirable bride possible—holy, cleansed, glorious.

Verse 28, *Thus husbands also are constantly obligated to keep on loving their wives as their own bodies. The one who keeps on loving his wife keeps on loving himself.* Paul's favorite comparative idea appears again. After the pattern of Christ's loving care for the church, the husband is to exercise loving care for his wife. The present tense of verbs, infinitives, and participles emphasizes the continued idea. They are under constant obligation to keep on loving their wives.

Paul continues this idea with the additional thought-provoking statement that such love is in a sense self-love, because the wife is a very part of the husband; the one who keeps on loving his own wife keeps on loving himself. It is not love and affection lavished upon an outsider. It is love and affection lavished upon one who is so dear as to be a part of one's own self.

Verses 29–30, *For no one ever hated his own flesh, but he cares for and cherishes it, just as Christ also (cherishes) the church, because members we are of his body.* Here Paul states that which is so common that it is regarded as axiomatic. No man hates his own flesh. Ideally, no man does that which will mean injury to his own body. In contrast, he gives particular care to his body. He cherishes it, answering its demands and its needs, taking care of it because of the evaluation which he places upon it. Paul honored the body and dignified the importance of it. In 1 Corinthians 6:19–20 he had said that the physical body of the Christian was the Holy Spirit's dwelling place here in the world. He said, too, that the total person, including the body, had been bought by the redemptive price of the blood of the Son of God. For this reason the body is to be used as a means of glorifying God. It is the normal thing for anyone to care for his own body. It is even more to be expected that the Christian is to care for his body.

Now Paul joins to that the idea that to love one's wife and to care for her is to love and to care for that which is a very part of himself. This, too, is followed by the statement concerning the pattern of Christ's caring for and cherishing his own body, which includes his own wife. Verse 30 perhaps suggests the additional idea that one who cares for his own wife is not only caring for his own body but is caring for a part of the body of Christ, because all Christians are members of that body. It is a Christian approach to domestic responsibility that man cherishes his wife as a part of the body for which Christ died.

Verse 31, *Facing this a man shall leave his father and his mother and shall be closely joined to his wife, and shall be the two unto one flesh.* This is Paul's use of Genesis 2:24. In typical fashion he goes back to the Hebrew Scriptures to find a basis for his teaching. That basis he finds in God's original purpose for man and woman. That original purpose was that the man should leave his father and his mother and establish his own home. He would be joined closely to his own wife. The verb translated "joined closely" very strictly rendered means "glued to." He is to be joined to his wife in such close relationship that the two of them come to be one flesh. This is a part of the mystery of marriage. It is a relationship in which man and wife come to be so closely related one to the other that they can in full truth be spoken of as one. It is this very oneness which makes for the appropriate expression of these mutual responsibilities. It is this oneness which causes the wife to subordinate herself to the husband in becoming fashion. It is this oneness which causes the husband so to love and cherish his wife that he gives up his own interest in order that her best interest may be advanced. Surely no higher concept of marriage and the home is to be found anywhere.

Verse 32, *This mystery is great, but I am speaking with reference to Christ and with reference to the church.* The entire area of thought relative to Christ and the church is a matter of mystery, that is, a matter which involves the principle of divine revelation. That is true where such lofty conception of marriage is involved. It is a matter which involves the necessity of divine revelation. It was a thing of mystery to Paul's readers that he should say that such devotion should be extended by any man to his wife. In the Gentile world that was an unheard-of concept. Even in the Jewish world, where woman had better standing, such a lofty concept was hardly to be found. In the Gentile world a woman was the property of her husband, and he could dispose of her as easily as he could dispose of any of the rest of his property. In the Jewish world a woman had a better standing than that, but in a practical sense she was still the property of her husband. When Paul said that the man is to exercise such loving care for his wife that he gives her interest first place and his own interest second place, he was indeed speaking a great mystery. He insists, however, that he is giving a distinctively Christian view of marriage. That is one of the wonders of revelation which God has given through the Christian religion.

Verse 33, *In summary, you also, each one, let him so love his own wife as himself, moreover the wife let her reverence the husband.* This closing verse of chapter 5 is the final summation of all that Paul has said about the wife's responsibility to the husband and the husband's responsibility to the wife. In one verse he restates all that responsibility, using a new word to describe the wife's attitude. He repeats what he has said to the effect that each man is constantly to love his own wife as he loves himself. She is a part of himself. Each wife, in turn, is to "reverence" her husband. Both the verb and the construction make for difficulty at this point. The verb is the word for fear. Certainly, it does not mean fear in the abject sense. Rather, it is fear in the sense of awe or reverence that is appropriate respect for the husband. The grammatical construction is that of a subjunctive which ordinarily expresses purpose, "the wife, in order that she reverence the husband." It appears in this use to have an unusual force equal to the third person imperative which was used of the husband. Let each husband *love* his wife; let each wife *reverence* her husband. In these two verbs the sum of mutual responsibility is expressed.

Duty of Child to Parent, 6:1–3

Paul next takes up another important area of domestic responsibility—the mutual responsibility of children and parents. This has a definite Jewish background, but it can hardly be improved upon as an expression of proper child-parent relationship. He speaks first of the responsibility of the child to the parent.

Verse 1, *Children, keep on obeying your parents in the Lord, for this is upright.* The generic use of the article again brings together all children and presents them as a class. This is the responsibility of all children. The imperative is in the present tense, speaking of continuous or habitual conduct—"keep on obeying" or "make a habit of obeying" your parents. The expression "in the Lord" relates this to the area of Christian responsibility. It perhaps is not to be understood as a simple qualifier of the word "parent" to the effect that children are to obey Christian parents. It is possible that that is the significance. It is possible that in some areas of the life of the day there were children who had become Christians while their parents had not embraced the Christian faith. In such cases Paul might be speaking of the responsibility of the child to show proper obedience to the Christian parent but leaving room for the exercise of practical wisdom in such cases where the parent had not embraced Christianity and might offer some objection to the child's giving expression to the principle of his new religion. Wherever responsibility to parent and responsibility to Christ would come into vital conflict, it is doubtful that Paul would advise the child to obey the parent.

Proper caution needs to be exercised in the application of this principle. We need to observe that we are speaking only of a possibility that Paul would give such instruction. It cannot be regarded as final. Again, one would need to exercise care in following such instruction to be sure that the interest of the parent was really in vital conflict with the Christian interest. Even such matters as the age and maturity of the children involved would have to be considered carefully. Most likely Paul is using this expression "in the Lord" to qualify the verb "obey." Ordinarily prepositional phrases qualify verbs. If that is the proper understanding, Paul is simply relating to the Christian area of conduct the obedience of the child to the parent. He would be carrying this beyond a simple parental responsibility in Jewish religious life. He would be saying that it is an expression of the Christian way of life for the child to exercise proper obedience to the parent.

Verses 2–3, *Honor your father and your mother, which is a commandment first in the realm of the promise, in order that well with you it may become and you shall be long of life upon the earth.* Again Paul goes to the Hebrew Scriptures for a passage to support his teaching. In this instance he combines Exodus 20:12 and Deuteronomy 5:16. The passage speaks of the responsibility of the child to show the attitude of honor or respect for parents. Again the verb is a present imperative which speaks of the necessity of continuous honoring of the parents.

This is the Commandment which stands out because of the promise related to it. Honor to father and mother held out the promise of well-being to the individual and the blessing of long life upon the earth. Proper understanding of all of this recognizes that there is no mechanical or arbitrary action involved here. It was not guaranteed that a person would live long in the world simply by giving proper honor to his parents. That was no magical formula for extending physical life. The idea was that proper respect for parents indicated a principle of right living, which within itself would promise well-being and the continuance of life.

Duty of Parent to Child, 6:4

In verse 4 Paul turns to the reciprocal relationship of the father to the child. This is not to be regarded as a one-way relationship. It is a matter of mutual relationship. Just as the child has the responsibility of obedience and honor to the parent, so the parent has a responsibility to the child.

Verse 4, *And fathers, stop provoking your children to wrath, but care for them in discipline and admonition of the Lord.* The responsibility of the father to the child is stated both negatively and positively. The generic use of the article embraces all fathers. The present imperative used in a negative command orders the cessation of conduct already in progress, "Fathers, stop enraging your children." The fathers are to conduct themselves in such way in relationship to the children that the children will be encouraged in exercising obedience and honor, rather than incited to retaliating outbursts of anger. This does not mean that the father is to allow the child to have his way uncontested when that way is wrong. In Hebrews 12:5–11 the writer says that God deals with disobedient children in the same way that the wise father deals with disobedient children, that is, he corrects them. This statement in Ephesians, then, is not to open the way to a "hands off" policy of the father in relationship to the child. It simply states that the father is to conduct himself in such way that he will not provoke his child to disobedience.

The positive side of the father's relationship to the child

is set out in the second part of the verse, "but care for them in discipline and admonition of the Lord." The word translated "care for" is an imperative. It speaks of the action of the father in bringing the child from infancy to maturity. Through all the years that the child is under the responsibility of the father, the father is to bring him up in the discipline and admonition of the Lord. The word translated "discipline" is the word for child instruction. It is the word which is used in the previously cited passage from Hebrews, in which the writer says that God disciplines his disobedient children in the same way that a wise father disciplines his disobedient children. The word translated "admonition" is the word basically related to the word for "mind." It was a word for "counsel." Proper discipline and proper counsel are to be the responsibilities of the parent in bringing the child to maturity. The word "Lord" appears to be in the ablative case, which would mean that this discipline and counsel have their source in the Lord himself. It may be that the word is in the genitive case as a descriptive term, that is, Lordly discipline and counsel. From either viewpoint the use of the word "Lord" gives a Christian tone to all that the father does in relationship to the child. He is not to provoke the child in such way as to encourage wrath or disobedience. He is rather to bring the child from infancy to maturity by means of Christian discipline and counsel. Need it be said further that the proper exercise of the mutual responsibilities of children and parents would go far toward correcting the tragic condition which exists today in contemporary home life?

Duty of Servant to Master, 6:5–8

Turning from the mutual responsibilities of immediate members of the family, Paul gives his attention to the application of the truth of redemption in Christ to the relationship between servants and masters. This, too, is an area where those who are in Christ must express the principles of Christian living with loyalty to the highest ideal. Just as the reality of Christianity reaches beyond the life of the individual and out into the area of his relationships within the home, so it reaches on to another circle of social life, and that is the circle which has to do with servants and masters and their mutual responsibilities as Christians. Paul takes up first the responsibility of the servant to the master. He devotes approximately three times as much space to the discussion of the duty of the servant as he does to the duty of the master. This is to be expected. The new spirit of liberty which was realized by those who came to experience redemption in Christ was likely to suffer abuse as those who were servants tried to give expression to a liberty which was new and strange. Paul's insistence is that the principles of the Christian life must be applied in the life of the servant as he addresses himself to the task which is given by his master.

Verse 5, *Servants, make a habit of obeying your master according to the flesh, with fear and trembling, in singleness of heart, as to the Lord.* This is a general principle by way of instruction. Later in verses 6 and 7 Paul will approach the subject from the familiar viewpoint of the negative and the positive. Here in verse 5, using again the generic article, he groups together all servants and uses the present imperative of continuous or habitual action to tell them that they are to obey their earthly masters. In reality the word which is translated "servants" means "bond servants" or "slaves." Apparently Paul was addressing himself to those who were slaves. The early leaders of the Christian movement did not take the approach of revolution in an attempt to bring a sudden change to all the social evils which existed in their day. Likely they realized that the new principle of liberty in Christ ultimately would bring about the breaking down of all barriers so that slavery could no longer be a part of a Christian society. They did not, however, try to bring an abrupt end to it. They gave instructions which would help at the point of right relationships between the owner and the owned.

Here the instruction is to servants who had become Christians. They were not to take the position that this new spiritual liberty which was theirs in Christ brought an end to their responsibilities in the social system of the day. They were, rather, to accept the challenge held out before them that being a Christian would make one a better worker in relationship even to human masters. The terms "fear" and "trembling" which characterized the obedience which they gave to their masters are terms that speak of proper reverence for the one who was their master and proper recognition that failure to perform their duties as servants would result in punishment from the master. Just because they were Christians they were not to think that they were exempt from the responsibilities which were theirs.

Another qualifier of their obedience to the masters is found in the expression "in singleness of your heart." Whereas the term "fear and trembling" might be looked upon as a negative motivation, this term "singleness of your heart" is altogether positive. It means "with sincerity," "without secondary or ulterior purpose." They recognized their obligations as servants, and they carried out those obligations in the most sincere way possible. The idea is further extended in the expression "as to Christ." This puts their obedience definitely into the framework of Christian motivation. While in the realm of the flesh they have earthly masters, in the realm of the spirit they have a heavenly Master—Christ. Because he is their Master, they are to give the very best possible effort in doing the work which is theirs here in this world. This is a most lofty motivation for sincere application to one's earthly responsibility.

Verse 6, *not according to eye service as men-pleasers, but as Christ's servants, doing the will of God from the soul.* Here again in striking parallel Paul suggests a negative approach to responsibility and a positive approach to responsibility. These Christian servants are not to do the work which their earthly master has assigned them "according to eye service as men-pleasers." This means literally that they are not to work only when the master is looking, having as their only motivation the doing of that which will please him. In contrast, the positive approach is observed in the statement that they are to serve as Christ's servants, doing continuously the will of God. They recognize a higher sense of ownership and obligation than the sense of earthly ownership. They belong to Christ. Because they belong to him, they are to do that which will be pleasing to him. While earthly masters cannot look on all the time to see that the servant does that which pleases them, God does look on all the time, and the service must be at all times pleasing to him. Furthermore, Paul says that this service is to be rendered "from the soul." Doubtless this is another means of emphasizing the spiritual motivation for the service which a Christian servant would render. His service is not one that is related just to the flesh so that the body moves as a machine to do that which is bidden. His service is to have the deepest thoughtful spiritual motivation from the very soul.

Verses 7–8, *with good will serving continually as to the Lord and not to men, knowing that each, if he do anything good, this he will receive back from the Lord whether serv-*

ant or free man. The word translated "good will" means "well-minded." Christian servants give attention to the service which they render, mindful of the fact that it is service which in the most real sense is rendered to the Lord and not just to men. Here is the stewardship of life, and here are the responsibilities of life. Few things can be more stabilizing and strengthening to the individual than the realization that he works not for a man or a group of men but in the last analysis he works for the eternal God. That recognition will be the supreme motivation for one's service, no matter what it is. If this is brought from the first century slave-master relationship over to the twentieth century employee-employer relationship, it becomes all the more meaningful. This means that no matter what one's position in life is as long as it is honest and honorable, he must do his best at that task simply because he is a Christian. It is no violence done to the principle involved in Paul's instruction if we say that a doctor will be a better doctor because he realizes that as a Christian doctor he must be at his best. A lawyer will be a better lawyer; a teacher will be a better teacher; a merchant will be a better merchant; a clerk will be a better clerk; a farmer will be a better farmer; a housewife will be a better housewife. All this may be summed up in this approach to responsibility, "I am a Christian; I must do my best."

In verse 8 Paul gives the Christians assurance that they do not lose if they give themselves to their task from this motivation of good service because they are Christians. He assures them that as they work they will realize that every individual will receive from the Lord recompense for whatever good he has done, whether he be a servant or a freeman. The Roman world was marked by great numbers of slaves. Many references to slaves appear in the New Testament. For instance, "those of Aristobulus" and "those of Narcissus" in Romans 16:10–11 were evidently groups of family slaves in Rome. Philemon was an owner of slaves, and one of his slaves who had run away, Onesimus, was converted to the Christian faith and sent back to his master by the apostle Paul (Philemon 9). There were also many freemen in the Roman world. These were people who had once been slaves but in one way or another had managed to become free. Paul's view is that no matter whether one is a slave or a freeman the Lord will reward him for his service. He will reward for service rendered and without partiality to both slave and freeman. The earthly servant is not to look to his earthly master for his ultimate reward for service; he is to look to his heavenly Master.

Duty of Master to Servant, 6:9

Following the previous pattern of expressing mutual responsibility of husband and wife and of parent and child, Paul now expresses the responsibility of earthly lords to their servants. Verse 9, *And masters, make a habit of doing the same things to them, leaving off threatening, knowing that both their Lord and yours is in heaven, and respect of persons is not with him.* Here as in the previous passages the generic use of the article groups all earthly masters into one body. Here again the present imperative is used to speak of the continual or habitual practice. Earthly masters are to conduct themselves habitually in the right manner with reference to their servants. They are to leave off threatening as a means of securing obedient service. Apparently, Paul's view is that Christian servants will respond to Christian masters who deal with them as human personalities who are able to measure up to the requirement of those who receive the right kind of treatment from their masters. Some servants may call for threats and penalties as a means of securing the right kind of service. Ideally, that is not true of the Christian. One who serves from Christian motivation will not require threat and penalty as an encouragement to do his work.

Paul's closing statement to the earthly masters is a reminder that even though they stand in a servant-master relationship to one another, here in this world both servants and masters have the same heavenly Master. This is further indication that Paul is addressing himself to servants and masters who are Christians. Both of them have the same heavenly Master. He is a heavenly Master who looks upon both of them as his servants. He does not look upon them primarily in their servant-master relationship to one another but in the relationship which they bear to him, and in that relationship they are both servants and he is the Master.

Paul assures them further that "respect of persons" is not with this heavenly Master. This is a most interesting word. It is a compound word made up of the noun meaning "face" and the verb meaning "to receive." It means then that the Lord in heaven does not look upon men according to their facial appearance; he does not receive men according to their facial appearance. The apostles learned this lesson in the days following Pentecost, when God granted salvation to Gentiles as well as to Jews. They came to see that God did not receive a man according to physical characteristics but according to spiritual characteristics. God receives no man according to facial appearances; he looks deeper than that.

In the ancient history of Israel the prophet Samuel learned that when he was sent of God to anoint one of the sons of Jesse to be king as successor to Saul. When Samuel saw Eliab, he thought that this tall, stately, handsome man must certainly be the one that God had chosen. God, however, told him not to look at the stature or the face of Eliab, because he was not God's chosen one. God then announced to Samuel a principle of evaluation which Christians today do well to observe, "The Lord sees not as man sees, for man looks on the outward appearance, but the Lord looks on the heart" (1 Sam. 16:7, RSV).

Twentieth-century Christians do well to apply this principle of divine evaluation in recognition of the fact that God does not receive men according to physical or external characteristics. He receives men according to their inner spiritual condition. In him there is no east or west, in him no north or south. In him there is no white or black or brown or red or yellow. His standard of evaluation and acceptance is a spiritual one. When man comes to recognize this truth, it means all the difference in the world in the expression of his own reactions to all his fellow men—slave or free, employer or employee. While this relationship of servants to masters is not an exact parallel of our relationship of employer and employee in twentieth-century social life and economy, it must be granted that if both employer and employee would devote themselves conscientiously to the principle which Paul sets out here, there would be far less difficulties and problems in employer-employee relationships. The application of genuine Christianity at any level is the best approach to a solution of mutual problems.

VI

Conclusion: The Fighting Saint

(6:10–20)

In Acts 28:16, 30 Luke tells that Paul spent two years as a prisoner in Rome, living in his own rented quarters and guarded by Roman soldiers. In Philippians 1:13 Paul reports that during this period of imprisonment he came to be acquainted with the entire Praetorian Guard. This was a group of soldiers whose particular responsibilty was guarding prisoners of the emperor. Paul was a prisoner of the emperor since he had appealed his case to the emperor's court. In this two years of contact with the Roman soldiers he doubtless heard much of their talk about their personal experiences, their enemies, their battles, their equipment, their victories. Alert to use the experiences of men in the illustration of spiritual truth, Paul seized upon the idea of the Christian life as a conflict with spiritual forces or evil. It is this idea which he carries out in most dramatic fashion as he nears the end of his treatment of basic Christianity. Basic Christianity inevitably comes into conflict with all the forces of evil, because it is diametrically opposed to all those forces. Paul views the Christian as a fighting saint. He encourages the Christian by reminding him that his ally is God; he alerts the Christian to the strong opposition in observing that his enemy is Satan himself; he urges the Christian to accept the equipment which God issues for all of those soldiers who fight in his army.

*His Ally—God, 6:10–11*a

Verses 10–11*a*, *Finally, be strengthened in the Lord, and in the power of his sufficiency. Put on the whole armor of God.* Paul begins at the most encouraging point by indicating that the ally of the fighting Christian is the Lord God himself. The Christian is to be strengthened in the Lord. This is the present passive imperative of the verb from which we derive our English word "endue." In the passive sense the verb meant to receive strength or to be strengthened by. It is in union with the Lord himself that this strength is realized. Further, it is indicated that the Christian is to be strengthened "in the power of his sufficiency." The pronoun "his" refers to the Lord. The Christian goes forth to do battle with the forces of evil, but he does not go in his own power or in his own sufficiency. He goes in the power and the sufficiency of the Lord God. Every Christian would have cause to waver as he looks at the tremendous enemy which is before him were it not for the fact that he recognizes that he goes not in his own sufficiency for the battle but in the sufficiency which is in the Lord and which the Lord gives to him.

The idea that God is the ally of the Christian in this battle is further carried out in the statement in verse 11 that the Christian is to put on the complete armor which God supplies. Just as in the Roman army the soldier received his equipment from his commanding officer, so in the Christian army the soldier receives his equipment from his commanding officer, God. The grammatical construction makes it clear that while God supplies the equipment or armor, it is the responsibility of the Christian to accept that equipment and to dress himself in it. When such equipment is furnished of God, how foolish would be that soldier who would go forth to battle without dressing himself in the armor provided.

*His Enemy—Satan, 6:11*b*–12*

The purpose of the Christian's dressing himself in the armor of God is introduced in the closing part of verse 11, *to be able you to stand, facing the cunning methods of the devil.* This is a very literal translation of the Greek text. The construction is that of an infinitive which expresses purpose. The Christian is to dress himself in the complete armor of God in order that he may be able to stand his ground when he faces the cunning devices of the devil. The word translated "cunning devices" would be transliterated from Greek into English by the word "methods." The devil, whose very name (slanderer) indicates his character as one that is deceitful, uses many cunning methods in carrying out his evil purposes among men. If the Christian soldier goes forth in his own sufficiency and improperly armed, he will be no match for Satan. If, however, he goes forth in the strength of the Lord, in the sufficiency of the Lord, and equipped with the armor which the Lord provides, he will be able to defeat the devil in spite of the many cunning methods which the devil uses.

Verse 12, *Because not is our struggle with blood and flesh, but with rulers, with authorities, with world powers of this darkness, with spiritual things of evil in the heavenlies.* This passage sets out clearly the nature of the battle and the nature of the enemy. The word which is translated "struggle" was the word for "hand-to-hand encounter." It might be used of two wrestlers in hand-to-hand struggle or of two soldiers who in the midst of battle faced off one against the other for a very personal hand-to-hand combat. This second idea appears to be the one that is used here. The enemy which the Christian soldier faces in personal face-to-face, hand-to-hand combat is not a flesh and blood enemy; rather, he is a spiritual enemy. The term "blood and flesh" was a term much used by the Jewish teachers to refer to man as a creature of frailty. Here it is used to make clear that the Christian's battle is not the battle against one who is only a man; it is a battle against one who exercises power which goes beyond human power.

Many efforts have been made to determine the particular meaning of the words which follow, "rulers, authorities, world powers of this darkness." Some interpreters have felt that these were used as references to governmental officers who were directing opposition against the cause of Christ by persecuting the Christians. They have felt that this is the correct interpretation because the terms were sometimes used for earthly rulers. That use here, however, would seem to reverse the entire emphasis which Paul desires to make. His assurance is that the enemy which the Christian faces is not a human enemy—governor, king, prince, or any other. Rather, the enemy that he faces is one of a spiritual nature. Many times Christians would find it easier to engage in battle if they had an enemy who was merely human, one who could feel the weight of fists or clubs or knives. That, however, is not the case. Their enemy is a spiritual enemy—Satan himself.

Paul appears to endorse the idea of a personal devil. In Ephesians 4:27 he told the Christians to stop giving a place to the devil. Here in 6:11 he speaks of the cunning devices of the devil, and in 6:16 he will speak of the fiery darts which the evil one shoots against the Christian soldier. If this brings about the idea of dualism, it must be noted that it is at the most a limited dualism. To deny the reality of the devil as a person appears to create more problems in the area of sin and suffering than are created by granting the reality of such a person. In verse 12 Paul says that the enemy of the Christians is a spiritual enemy of evil character "in the heavenlies." This word "heavenlies" is used five times in this epistle. It always has to do with that which is higher than, or goes beyond, the natural. Satan, who is the highest enemy of God, is by that same token the highest enemy of God's soldiers.

His Equipment—Full Armor, 6:13–20

Paul begins this specific discussion of the Christian armor by using a causal clause. Because of the spiritual nature of the opposition, the Christian soldier must have spiritual equipment for this spiritual battle. Verse 13, *On account of this take up the complete armor of God, in order that you may be enabled to stand against (the enemy) in the evil day, and having done everything to stand (at attention).* Paul repeats the idea which he had expressed in verse 11, that God supplies the complete equipment which his soldier will need in this spiritual battle. The word translated "whole armor" or "complete equipment" is transliterated into English "panoplia." The Greek adjective *pan,* meaning "all" or "complete," is quite evident in the word. God does not send his soldier into battle partially equipped; he provides for him complete equipment. It is the responsibility of the soldier to take up this equipment and to use it in battle.

The purpose of his taking up this complete equipment is set out in the next clause, "in order that you may be enabled to stand against (the enemy) in the evil day." With this equipment the soldier will be able to hold his own in battle. The term "stand against" is a compound form of the verb meaning "to stand" and the preposition meaning "against" or "facing." "The evil day" apparently means the time when the forces of evil are at their peak of operation. At such time the Christian soldier, completely equipped with the armor which God has supplied, will be able to stand his ground in battle. More than that, when he has completed and won any particular battle, he will be in a position of standing at attention, ready for the commanding officer's next order. That appears to be Paul's meaning in the expression "having done all things to stand."

*Girdle—Truth, 6:14*a

In verse 14 Paul takes up piece by piece the equipment which was supplied the soldier in the Roman army. He assigns a spiritual significance to each piece as it has its counterpart in the armor which God provides for his soldier. The soldier who has all this equipment lacks nothing.

Verse 14, *Take your stand, therefore, having wrapped around your loins in truth.* The participle translated "having wrapped around" was the word for the girdle which was worn by the Roman soldier. This was a broad belt of leather and metal or cloth and metal, and it served for him a double purpose. It gave to him a sense of support which prevented his growing weary in battle, and it was used for securing to his person other parts of his equipment, such as the sword or perhaps even the smaller shield which the soldier sometimes used. In allegorical fashion Paul holds that it is truth which serves this double purpose for the Christian soldier. Truth doubtless means, here as elsewhere in the New Testament, the truth of God as it is revealed in the Christian religion. It is this truth which gives strength to the soldier and prevents his growing weary in conflict. At the same time it is this truth which keeps all the Christian soldier's equipment properly organized and ready for use.

Just think what tragedy it would be today if in some television program the shining hero reached for his gun only to find that it had slipped around beyond his reach! There would be the end of a good TV program! By the same token, the Roman soldier had to find his sword in place when he reached for it. Truth, like the Roman soldier's girdle, keeps all the Christian soldier's equipment in proper place for effective use.

*Breastplate—Righteousness, 6:14*b

And having put on the breastplate of righteousness. The breastplate of the Roman soldier was for the protection of the vital organs—heart, lungs, throat, etc. That which gives protection to the vital organs of the Christian soldier is genuine righteousness. The word "righteousness" means uprightness. Elsewhere in Paul's letters it is used as a characteristic of God. It is also used as a description of the person who links himself to God by faith in Jesus Christ. Such a one God makes to be upright, partaking of his own righteous character. It is this righteousness which protects for the Christian that which is most vital. The finest thing that God does for any person is to make that person good or righteous. The realization of the possession of this quality is a necessary part of the armor of that one who would do battle with the forces of evil. Without this righteousness he will be as vulnerable as is the opposition. With this righteousness he has protection from God himself.

Sandals—Readiness, 6:15

And having sandaled your feet in readiness of the gospel of peace. The word "sandal" is not properly a verb. The verb which Paul uses means literally "to bind under," that is, "having bound under your feet" in readiness of the gospel of peace. The Roman soldier wore hobnailed sandals. When he engaged in hand-to-hand conflict, no matter how slippery the ground, he was able to stand because of these hobnailed sandals. Paul suggests that God supplies sandals for his soldiers. God provides that which will make it possible for the Christian soldier to hold his ground in the conflict with evil. The word which he uses for the Christian sandals may be translated "preparation" or "readiness." "Readiness" appears to be a better word for the idea that Paul desires to express. Readiness in relationship to the gospel of peace, a burning readiness or preparation for whatever one faces in spiritual conflict—this is the equipment which serves like hobnailed sandals for holding one's own against opposition.

Shield—Faith, 6:16

In everything having taken up the shield of faith, with which you will be able all the fiery darts of the evil one to quench. Students of Greek will notice that the word translated "shield" is related to the Greek word for door. The shield that Paul has in mind here was not the small, round one but rather the large, rectangular shield. The small, round shield might be carried in the performance of one's duties where no emergency was involved. When the real battle started, however, the Roman soldier wanted the large, rectangular shield and the protection that it alone could give. Some of the enemies of the Romans had developed the predecessor of modern incendiary warfare. They dipped their arrows in pitch and set fire to them before shooting them into the bodies of the enemy. To offset the effectiveness of these arrows the Romans developed a shield made of alternating layers of bronze and oxhide. These shields were strong enough to break the force of the fiery arrows and to cause them to fall harmlessly to the ground. Paul conceives of Satan as one who fires burning arrows at the Christian. What is the Christian's shield against such burning arrows? It is faith. No matter how thick the arrows nor how much they flame, faith is able to compete with them, turning them to one side or causing them to fall to the ground, spent and ineffective. Whatever Satan's fiery arrows, whether of doubt or of discouragement, the Christian can compete with them by means of the shield which God provides—faith.

*Helmet—Salvation, 6:17*a

And receive the helmet of salvation. The helmet which the Roman soldier used was for the protection of his head. It appears a strange idea that Paul should speak of salvation as the helmet for the Christian. Ordinarily, we think of salvation in terms of that which is related to the heart more than that which is related to the head. Perhaps we do well to stop and consider Paul's suggestion that the entire mental process of man is involved in this matter of salvation. Salvation, that is, deliverance from the powers of evil, is to have its effective work in the area of man's rational life as well as in every other area of life.

In the Old Testament story of Job one follows the progress of God's conversation with Satan with great interest. There was a day when Satan appeared before God, and in response to God's question about his conduct he indicated that he had been going to and fro in the earth, carrying out the evil which was related to his true character. God asked if Satan had noted Job and his loyalty to God. Satan's reply was a rather scornful one to the effect that he had noted Job and his loyalty but he was of the opinion that Job's loyalty would be a different matter were it not for the protection which God offered. Satan told God that if God would remove that protection and let him work on Job a bit he would prove that Job served God for a reason. God told Satan to do what he would, only he was not to touch the person of Job.

In the story it is told that Satan went to work with the disastrous result of the loss to Job of his camels, of his sheep, of his other livestock, even of his children. Still he remained loyal to God. The next time God and Satan discussed Job Satan had to admit that Job was still loyal to God, but, continuing with his excuses, he insisted that Job was loyal because he had not been touched personally. It was Satan's view that if he could get his hands upon Job's person he would show God that Job really wasn't loyal at all. Then it was that God told Satan, "Behold, he is in your hand, only spare his life" (Job 2:6). Satan went forth from the presence of God to smite Job with boils and to bring him to such miserable state that even Job's wife recommended that he renounce God and die. Job, however, insisted that he would receive both good and evil without revolting against what seemed to be God's providential dealing with him.

Ordinarily we understand that what God was saying to Satan was: "Do what you wish to Job, only do not kill him. As long as Job has life he will be loyal to me." That is a beautiful thought, and it may be exactly what is meant. It is possible, however, to translate the passage, "He is in your hand, only spare his reason." By this rendering God would be saying to Satan, "As long as Job is in his right mind he will be loyal to me." That, too, is a beautiful tribute and a truthful one. Salvation, then, as the helmet for the Christian soldier, may be the indication that all the Christian's rational powers are dedicated to God and used in the conflict with evil.

*Sword—God's Word, 6:17*b

And (*receive*) *the sword of the Spirit, which is God's word.* This appears to be the only offensive weapon in the

Christian's equipment. Some have understood that the helmet was both offensive and defensive since the Roman soldier made himself look taller and more formidable to his enemy by wearing a tall, plumed helmet! Most likely, however, the helmet was—along with the shield, the sandals, the breastplate, and the girdle—a weapon for the defense of the soldier. The one weapon of offense for the Christian soldier is the sword which the Holy Spirit supplies and which the Holy Spirit uses, that is, God's Word. The term which is translated "word" means "the thing said." This recalls the experience of Jesus in the wilderness when he met the temptation of Satan by using quotations from the Hebrew Scriptures. The "thing said" of God is the Christian's best weapon of offense as he faces Satan in spiritual conflict. Some interpreters understand "the word of God" here to mean the preached word or the gospel. That may well be. The good news of God in Christ on a mission of destroying the works of evil is the Christian's most effective implement of battle.

Paul concludes this effective picture of the fighting saint with encouragement that the Christian shall undergird his use of all this equipment by prayer and supplication. Verse 18, *by means of all prayer and petition, praying in the Spirit on every occasion, and always watching in all steadfastness and petition concerning all the saints.* As the Christian soldier takes up his armor, he takes up each piece with prayer that he shall use it in the most effective way. This he does on every occasion of battle. On every occasion he prays that he shall use the armor effectively, and he prays in the ever watchful attitude of one who carries in his heart not only his own interest but those of all his fellow soldiers in battle.

In verse 19 Paul urges that these Ephesian Christians, as they engage prayerfully in the spiritual conflict of life, praying that they shall use aright the Lord's equipment, shall include him, too, in their prayers. Verses 19–20, *and in behalf of me, in order that to me may be given utterance in opening my mouth, to make known in boldness the mystery of the gospel, on behalf of which I am an ambassador in chains, in order that in it I may speak boldly as I ought to speak.* Even though Paul is now a prisoner, he is still, with the Ephesians, a fighting saint. He is serving as an ambassador, though an ambassador in chains. An ambassador is one who represents a government at some foreign court. Paul was God's representative, and even in his chains he felt constrained to carry out his work as an ambassador. He requested that the Christians who read this letter would include him in their prayers. He asked that they pray for him in order that utterance might be given to him to proclaim with perfect freedom of speech the mystery of the gospel.

The gospel mystery was that God in Christ had provided redemption for all men without regard to race, and this redemption made all who received it one spiritual body in Christ. Even though Paul had become a prisoner because of preaching that wonderful news, he could not refrain from continuing that preaching. That was the very heart of the Christian religion—one God providing one way of redemption for all men and making of all the redeemed one spiritual body of which Christ is the head. That, in the final analysis, is *basic Christianity*. That, in the final analysis, is the issue over which the entire battle between the Christian soldier and Satan himself was being fought in Paul's day and is being fought in our own day. What tremendous courage comes to the Christian soldier who realizes that in this battle he is fighting on the side of the eternal God. That means that victory is his ultimate destiny.

Farewell

(6:21–24)

The closing words of this letter to the Christians in Asia Minor had particular meaning for those who first received the letter. Paul assured the readers that one beloved to him and to them, a faithful minister in the Lord, Tychicus, would inform them of all his affairs and would comfort them with the assurance that even though Paul was a prisoner all was well with him. He was so concerned lest they be anxious about him that he was sending Tychicus for the specific purpose of informing the Christians in Asia Minor of his experience and condition.

The letter closes with the same wish of grace and peace which opened it. Peace is joined to love and faith as a blessing which Paul pronounced upon his Christian brethren. This peace, love, and faith had their source in God the Father and the Lord Jesus Christ. The blessing of grace, God's own favor, is extended to all those who love the Lord Jesus Christ with an undying love. This is typical of Paul. Not all of his letters were so filled with good news, commendation, and blessing as was this Ephesian letter. He was sometimes harsh as occasion demanded, such as he was in writing Galatians and parts of 1 and 2 Corinthians. He was sometimes the very essence of gentleness, as in his letter to his favorite church at Philippi. Whatever the nature of his letters, he could always, in the spirit of the Christ that he loved, close with a benediction and expression of grace to those who received the letter. How impoverished Christianity would be without these letters from the pen of this great apostle! How very impoverished Christianity would be particularly without this expression of the very basic elements that make up Christianity!

Bibliography

Background and Introduction

BARNETT, ALBERT E. *The New Testament: Its Making and Meaning.* New York: Abingdon-Cokesbury Press, 1956.

BARON, SALO W., AND BLAU, JOSEPH L. (eds.). *Judaism.* New York: The Liberal Arts Press, 1954.

CARMICHAEL, PATRICK H. (ed.). *Understanding the Books of the New Testament.* Richmond: John Knox Press, 1952.

CARTLEDGE, SAMUEL A. *A Conservative Introduction to the New Testament.* Grand Rapids: Zondervan Publishing House, 1938.

CUMONT, FRANZ. *The Mysteries of Mithra.* New York: Dover Publications, Inc., 1956.

DANA, H. E. *The Life and Literature of Paul.* Chicago: Blessing Book Stores, Inc., 1937.

DAUBE, DAVID. *The New Testament and Rabbinic Judaism.* University of London: The Athlone Press, 1956.

DAVIES, W. D., AND DAUBE, D. (eds.). *The Background of the New Testament and Its Eschatology.* Cambridge: University Press, 1956.

DUNCAN, GEORGE S. *St. Paul's Ephesian Ministry.* New York: Charles Scribner's Sons, 1930.

FILSON, FLOYD V. *Opening the New Testament.* Philadelphia: The Westminster Press, 1952.

FOWLER, HENRY THATCHER. *The History and Literature of the New Testament.* New York: The Macmillan Company, 1934.

FRASER, IAN W. *Understanding the New Testament.* New York: Abingdon-Cokesbury Press, 1956.

GOODSPEED, EDGAR J. *Christianity Goes to Press.* New York: The Macmillan Company, 1940.

———. *A History of Early Christian Literature.* Chicago: The University of Chicago Press, 1942.

———. *How Came the Bible?* New York: Abingdon-Cokesbury Press, 1940.

———. *An Introduction to the New Testament.* Chicago: The University of Chicago Press, 1937.

———. *The Key to Ephesians.* Chicago: The University of Chicago Press, 1956.

———. *New Chapters in New Testament Study.* New York: The Macmillan Company, 1937.

GOODWIN, FRANK J. *A Harmony of the Life of St. Paul.* New York: American Tract Society, n.d.

GRANT, FREDERICK C. *An Introduction to New Testament Thought.* New York: Abingdon-Cokesbury Press, 1950.

——— (ed.). *Hellenistic Religions.* New York: The Liberal Arts Press, 1953.

HAYES, D. A. *Paul and His Epistles.* New York: The Methodist Book Concern, 1915.

HEARD, RICHARD. *An Introduction to the New Testament.* New York: Harper & Brothers Publishers, 1950.

KEE, HOWARD CLARK, AND YOUNG, FRANKLIN W. *Understanding the New Testament.* New Jersey: Prentice-Hall Inc., 1957.

KENYON, FREDERICK G. *Handbook to the Textual Criticism of the New Testament.* Grand Rapids: Wm. B. Eerdmans Publishing Company, 1951.

KNOX, JOHN. *Chapters in a Life of Paul.* New York: Abingdon-Cokesbury Press, 1946.

LAKE, KIRSOPP AND SILVA. *An Introduction to the New Testament.* New York: Harper & Brothers Publishers, 1937.

MITTON, CHARLES LESLIE. *The Epistle to the Ephesians.* New York: Oxford Press, 1952.

———. *The Formation of the Pauline Corpus of Letters.* London: The Epworth Press, 1955.

MOE, OLAF. *The Apostle Paul: His Life and His Work.* Minneapolis: Augsburg Publishing House, 1950.

MORTON, H. V. *In the Steps of St. Paul.* New York: Dodd, Mead & Company, 1942.

PEAKE, ARTHUR S. *A Critical Introduction to the New Testament.* New York: Charles Scribner's Sons, 1920.

RIDDLE, DONALD W., AND HUTSON, HAROLD H. *New Testament Life and Literature.* Chicago: The University of Chicago Press, 1946.

ROBERTSON, A. T. *An Introduction to the Textual Criticism of the New Testament.* Nashville: Sunday School Board of the Southern Baptist Convention, 1925.

ROWLINGSON, DONALD T. *Introduction to New Testament Study.* New York: The Macmillan Company, 1956.

Interpretation

BEARE, FRANCIS W., AND WEDEL, THEODORE O. *The Epistle to the Ephesians* (*The Interpreter's Bible,* Vol. 10.) Nashville: Abingdon-Cokesbury Press, 1953.

CALVIN, JOHN. *Commentaries on the Epistles of Paul to the Galatians and Ephesians.* Grand Rapids: Wm. B. Eerdmans Publishing Company, 1948.

CARVER, WILLIAM OWEN. *The Glory of God in the Christian Calling.* Nashville: Broadman Press, 1949.

CONYBEARE, W. J., AND HOWSON, J. S. *The Life and Epistles of St. Paul.* Grand Rapids: Wm. B. Eerdmans Publishing Company, 1949.

EADIE, JOHN. *Commentary on the Epistle to the Ephesians.* Grand Rapids: Zondervan Publishing House, n.d.

EERDMAN, CHARLES R. *The Epistle of Paul to the Ephesians.* Philadelphia: The Westminster Press, 1931.

FAUSSET, A. R. *Commentary on 1 Corinthians—Revelation* (*A Critical, Experimental, and Practical Commentary on the Old and New Testaments,* Vol. VI.) Grand Rapids: Wm. B. Eerdmans Publishing Company, 1945.

LENSKI, R. C. H. *The Interpretation of St. Paul's Epistles to the Galatians, to the Ephesians, and to the Philippians.* Columbus: The Wartburg Press, 1937.

LOCK, WALTER. *The Epistle to the Ephesians* (*The Westminster Commentaries.*) London: Methuen and Company, Ltd., 1929.

MACKAY, JOHN A. *God's Order.* New York: The Macmillan Company, 1953.

MOULE, H. C. G. *Ephesian Studies.* New York: G. P. Putnam's Sons, 1900.

MULLINS, E. Y. *Studies in Ephesians and Colossians.* Nashville: Sunday School Board of the Southern Baptist Convention, 1913.

REIKE, BO. *The Disobedient Spirits and Christian Baptism.* Kobenhaven: Ejnar Munksgaard, 1946.

SALMOND, S. D. F. *The Epistle to Second Corinthians, Galatians, Ephesians, Philippians, and Colossians* (*The Expositor's Greek Testament,* Vol. III.) Grand Rapids: Wm. B. Eerdmans Publishing Company, n.d.

SIMPSON, E. K., AND BRUCE, F. F. *Commentary on the Epistles to the Ephesians and the Colossians* (*The New International Commentary on the New Testament.*) Grand Rapids: Wm. B. Eerdmans Publishing Co., 1957.

SMITH, DAVID. *The Life and Letters of St. Paul.* New York: Harper & Brothers Publishers, n.d.

SMITH, JUSTIN A. *Commentary on Corinthians to Thessalonians* (*An American Commentary on the New Testament,* Vol. V.) Philadelphia: The American Baptist Publication Society, 1887.